THE LATIN IMAGE IN AMERICAN FILMS

A Book on Lore

UCLA LATIN AMERICAN STUDIES

Volume 39

Series Editor

Johannes Wilbert

The Latin Image in American Film

Allen L. Woll

UCLA Latin American Center Publications
University of California   Los Angeles
1977

UCLA LATIN AMERICAN CENTER PUBLICATIONS

University of California, Los Angeles

Copyright © 1977 by The Regents of the University of California

All rights reserved

Library of Congress Catalog Card Number: 77-620044

ISBN: 0-87903-039-9

Printed in the United States of America

Grateful acknowledgment is made for permission to print the following:

Lyrics: SHE COULD SHAKE THE MARACAS (Richard Rodgers and Lorenz Hart). Copyright © 1939 by Chappell & Co., Inc. Copyright renewed. All rights reserved. Used by permission of Chappell & Co., Inc. SIGH NO MORE (Noël Coward). Copyright © 1945 by Chappell & Co., Ltd. Copyright renewed. All rights reserved. Used by permission of Chappell & Co., Ltd. SHE'S A LATIN FROM MANHATTAN (Al Dubin and Harry Warren). Copyright © 1935 Warner Bros. Inc. Copyright renewed. All rights reserved. Used by permission. CHICA CHICA BOOM CHIC (Harry Warren and Mack Gordon). Copyright © 1941, renewed 1968, 20th Century Music Corp. Rights throughout the world controlled by Miller Music Corp. Used by permission. GOOD NIGHT, GOOD NEIGHBOR (Frank Loesser and Arthur Schwartz). Copyright © 1943 Warner Bros. Inc. Copyright renewed. All rights reserved. Used by permission.

Photographs: Paul Muni in BORDERTOWN. Courtesy Wisconsin Center for Film and Theater Research. Paul Muni in JUAREZ. Courtesy Wisconsin Center for Film and Theater Research. Dolores Del Rio and Ricardo Cortez in WONDER BAR. Courtesy Wisconsin Center for Film and Theater Research. Dolores Del Rio in IN CALIENTE. Courtesy Wisconsin Center for Film and Theater Research. Carmen Miranda in THE GANG'S ALL HERE. Copyright © 1943 Twentieth Century-Fox Film Corporation. All rights reserved. Betty Grable in DOWN ARGENTINE WAY. Copyright © 1940 Twentieth Century-Fox Film Corporation. All rights reserved. WINGED VICTORY. Copyright © 1944 Twentieth Century-Fox Film Corporation. All rights reserved. Marlon Brando and Jean Peters in VIVA ZAPATA! Copyright © 1952, 20th Century-Fox Film Corporation. All rights reserved.

ACKNOWLEDGMENTS

Motion picture history is a difficult field to research. The films discussed herein are scattered throughout the country and I would like to thank those who made these prints available. Susan Dalton and the staff of the University of Wisconsin Center for Theater Research provided access to all the RKO and Warner Brothers films. Without their cooperation, I could never have completed this book. Thomas O'Brien, Sr., and Thomas O'Brien, Jr., graciously provided Columbia films for my viewing. The Library of Congress Film Division and Films Incorporated of Skokie, Illinois, allowed me to see the MGM films that I have discussed.

Special thanks are due Lois Drapin, Reid Andrews, and Ramón Gutiérrez for reading parts of the manuscript and offering their comments. Peter H. Smith, John L. Phelan, and Thomas E. Skidmore of the University of Wisconsin, Madison, and Simon Collier of the University of Essex, Great Britain, encouraged my interest in Latin America and their contribution is greatly appreciated.

CONTENTS

Illustrations between pages 52 and 53

ABBREVIATIONS

Following the first mention of each silent film the date of release is included in parentheses. For each sound film, the producer and date of release is included. The following abbreviations are used:

Col	Columbia
CUE	Commonwealth United Entertainment
MGM	Metro-Goldwyn-Mayer
Par	Paramount
RKO	RKO Radio Pictures
20th	Twentieth Century–Fox
UA	United Artists
Univ	Universal
WB	Warner Brothers

1

INTRODUCTION

Every Latin has a temper
Latins have no brain.
And they quarrel as they walk in
Latin Lover's Lane.

"She Could Shake the Maracas"
in *Too Many Girls**

America's minorities are at last coming into their own on the motion picture screen. Blacks have graduated from their janitorial jobs of World War II films and now portray doctors, lawyers, and physicists. The American Indian is no longer the barbarous villain who attacks helpless white settlers. In such films as *Little Big Man* and *Soldier Blue,* the destruction of Indian culture and society is finally revealed. The Oriental is no longer the shuffling coolie, the sinister Fu Manchu, or a Confucian Charlie Chan. The Kung Fu films have single-handedly smashed the myth of Oriental submissiveness on the screen.

1

Only the Latin American has missed the cultural reorientation of the films of the past decade. With such motion pictures as *Bring Me the Head of Alfredo Garcia, Bananas, Viva Max!,* and *The Good, The Bad, and the Ugly,* the Latin has remained a rapacious bandit or an object of ridicule.[1] Even more degrading is the fact that a Latin is rarely able to portray his own race in leading film roles. The practice of whites portraying blacks disappeared soon after *The Birth of a Nation* in 1915. The white Oriental, such as Boris Karloff's Fu Manchu, is now a thing of the past. In recent years, however, the major Latin roles have gone to Peter Ustinov, Rod Steiger, Eli Wallach, and Marlon Brando. None of these gentlemen hail from further south than the Mason-Dixon Line.

Whenever Latins do portray themselves, one thing is clear: the accent remains on violence. The spaghetti Western, the Sam Peckinpah films, or even *Butch Cassidy and the Sundance Kid* paint a culture founded on bloodshed and death. "The Revolution" becomes the most familiar image of South American life in the films of recent years. Yet, rarely is there a cause or a goal in this social upheaval. As Rod Steiger reveals in *Duck, You Sucker,* all that matters is murder and destruction.

Americans thus receive a dominant picture of Latin society populated by murderous *banditos* and submissive, but sensual, peasant women. Unfortunately, there is little to balance this all-too-prevalent stereotype. Television news avoids Latin America, except in the case of the latest revolution. Books concerning Latin America are rarely popular. As Walter Lippmann once noted, "Americans would do anything for Latin America except read about it." Even popular songs emphasize the image of the happy-go-lucky *caballero* who is only interested in love. As a result, the film remains the predominant source of U.S. perceptions of South America. And, if this is the case, the film image of the Latin and his society bears little relation to the current realities of the Continent.

Unfortunately, there is nothing new in this confused representation of the vast territory south of the Río Grande. From the beginning of the Spanish Conquest in 1492, the Europeans found the New World a strange and barbarous land, especially in the tropical climes. Vegetation was lush and exotic, animal life was of unknown varieties, and the inhabitants were the most curious of all. An early voyager claimed that the natives "had square heads and were colored blue." Since the Indians despised their blue skin color, this traveler reasoned that they painted themselves red.[2]

An artist who accompanied Amerigo Vespucci on his third voyage found the natives singularly barbaric beings who "hung human flesh in their homes in order to dry it." These heathens often reached the age of one hundred and fifty years, and they rarely became ill. The men and women often grew to giant size, and occasionally Indians with tails were discovered.[3]

These early travelers might be forgiven their occasional excesses. Arriving on the new continent in the sixteenth century might be likened to a landing on Mars today. Both are strange and exotic lands where anything might be expected. Unfortunately, the conquistadores, their military troops, and the early settlers had few scientists among them. The men of learning resided in Europe and analyzed the New World from the accounts of these untrained observers.

The men of science of the Enlightenment had two and a half centuries of reports from the Americas on which to base their generalizations. Their uniform conclusion found South America a hopelessly decadent continent. The Abbé Raynal noted in his *Philosophical and Political History of the Settlements and Trade of Europeans in the Two Indies (1770–1772)* that "everything in the New World exhibits the vestiges of a malady of which the human race still feels the effects. The ruin of that world is still imprinted on its inhabitants. They are a species of men degraded and degenerated in their natural constitution, in their stature, in their way of life, and in their understanding, which is but little advanced in all the arts of civilization."[4]

As Raynal finished his tract on the New World, he invited the Academy of Lyon to discuss the question "Was the discovery of America a blessing or a curse for mankind?" He donated a large sum of money as a prize for the best essay, and he invited the top scientists of Europe to compete. The essays differentiated between North and South America, finding the temperate climes the cradle of future scientific progress, while dismissing the tropical areas as hopeless backwaters.

Their analyses of the inhabitants of South America reveal ambiguous stereotypes of the Latin American personality which persist in Western thought today. The South American males were the most enigmatic to these men of learning. On one hand, the men were weak and impotent: "In the savage the organs of generation are small and feeble. He has no hair, no beard, and no desire for the female. His sensations are less acute, and yet he is more cowardly and timid."[5] Yet, beneath this calm exterior, the Latins were prone to extremes of violence, most notably in their penchant for cannibalistic behavior. The Aztecs indulged in human sacrifice, and the aborigines of Brazil and Chile ate their captives in war. The moral was that the Latin American could not be trusted, for his surface pacificity disguised an uncontrollable inner violence.

The women, however, were different. Sensual and exotic, they were often attractive to the early settlers. Their fecundity was notorious. A credulous Dutch traveler happened upon a Brazilian woman breast-feeding her children in a jungle den. His immediate assumption was that the native was *growing* the infants from her chest! Only in this manner could the prolific Latin woman produce so many children.[6] The women, in addition to being more sensual than the male, were often depicted as more powerful than their husbands. The mythical Brazilian Amazons reveal this tendency. These giant women were the warriors, while their placid husbands remained at home to tend the children and prepare the food for dinner.[7]

Again, these savants of the Enlightenment Age might be excused for their exaggerations, since none had even approached the New World shores. In the present century, though, there is no further excuse for the stereotypical versions of the Latin that appear in our popular mythology. From the Frito Bandito to

Chiquita Banana, views of Latin men and women have remained static since 1900. Nowhere is this more true than on the American screen where the dated conceptions of the Middle Ages and the Enlightenment rather than the current realities of the South American continent shape the filmic image of the Latin American. Hopefully, this analysis of the Latin image in American film will reveal the continuance of these misconceptions in American popular culture and lead to their eradication.

NOTES

1. These films are discussed in Chapter 7.

2. The literature on European views of America is extensive. See Antonello Gerbi, *La disputa del nuevo mundo* (Mexico City, 1960) and Hugh Honor, *The New Golden Land* (New York, 1976).

3. M. A. Rojas Mix, *La imagen artística de Chile* (Santiago, Chile, 1970), Chap. I.

4. Henry Steele Commager and Elmo Giordanetti, *Was America a Mistake? An Eighteenth-Century Controversy* (Columbia, S.C., 1967), pp. 125–131.

5. Ibid., pp. 13–15.

6. Gerbi, *La disputa,* pp. 42–48.

7. Rojas, Mix, *La imagen artística,* pp. 63–64.

2

THE ATTACK
OF THE
GREASERS

THE LATIN IMAGE IN SILENT FILMS
1894–1928

> Imagination in the production of motion pic-
> tures has clothed the men from the other
> Americas with a mental and material garb
> which only belong in the property room of a
> touring musical comedy.
>
> Miguel Cruchaga Tocornal, Chilean Ambassador
> to the United States.
> *New York Times,* April 3, 1927

The Early Years

The new cinematic medium introduced American audiences to
images of the world around them. People who had never left
their native Brooklyn or Boston might visually attend the coro-
nation of a czar, travel down the Nile River, or visit the French
Riviera. These early films presented a documentary view of
foreign cultures to American viewers.

The first sights of Latin America in the local peep shows and
nickelodeons were often dominated by the classic Spanish
ritual of the bullfight. Before 1900 this manly sport became
the prime cultural characteristic of Mexico in American minds.

The emphasis on the bullfight was partly accidental. In 1896, Enoch J. Rector abandoned an attempt to film a boxing match in Texas owing to legal difficulties. He moved the bout to Mexico and set up his cameras in preparation for the fight. Rain intervened, so in order to avoid a total loss, Rector's crew moved to Juarez and filmed a bullfight.[1]

The unexpected popularity of this film led the Edoloscope Company, headed by Major Woodville Latham, to send a crew southward for the specific purpose of filming a bullfight. Latham sent his son, Otway, on the expedition, advising him to also try to film "the rites of the Flagellantes in annual presentation of a half-savage version of the Passion Play." Otway was unable to film this unusual passion play, but did manage to film the bullfight, although the recalcitrant bull habitually ran out of the viewer's range. While the filming was accomplished virtually without difficulties, Otway faced a problem that has plagued film crews to the present day. An overzealous customs inspector insisted on opening the cans of undeveloped film. Although a majority of the film was ruined, enough was salvaged to be shown in New York and "draw considerable crowds" in its initial screening.[2]

By the turn of the century, the travelogues of the early years were abandoned as the silent films with plots came into vogue. In the nineteenth century only one story film concerning Mexico was made. The 1894 Edison Kinetoscope catalogue advertised *Pedro Esquirel and Dionecio Gonzales: Mexican Duel,* a forty-foot film described as "full of action, exciting, and interesting."[3] By 1900, the exception became the rule, and the plot was deemed of paramount importance.

These new films at last introduced American audiences to their nearby Mexican neighbors, and no doubt they were shocked by what they saw. Although the majority of early silent films emphasized action and violence, the Mexican bandits were clearly among the most vile. They robbed, murdered, plundered, raped, cheated, gambled, lied, and displayed virtually every vice that could be shown on the screen.

As a reward for the Mexican's degraded state, he achieved a new name. He was not known as a Mexican, or even an Indian, but was dubbed "the greaser," one of the screen's most despicable characters. Hence, even the titles of such films as *Tony the Greaser* (1911), *Broncho Billy and the Greaser* (1914), and *The Greaser's Revenge* (1914) revealed an innate prejudice against the Mexican.

The typical "greaser" was violent and prone to murder, as Broncho Billy discovered when he met his first greaser in 1914:

Broncho Billy, the mail carrier, ejects a greaser from the post office for pushing a girl out of the way. The half-breed is thoroughly angered and swears revenge. Billy then goes home and on the way he loses his mailbag. He does not miss it, so he goes to bed that night unaware of his loss. The girl he protected at the post office finds the mail bag, and when she approaches Billy's shack to return it, she sees the greaser prowling about. She hastens to a dance hall, where she tells her friends of Broncho's danger, and she leads the way back to his shack where they arrive just in time to save him from being stabbed while asleep.[4]

While the normal villain would primarily murder or steal, the Mexican greaser often carried his occupation to excess. More often than not, he enjoyed his subtle extension of the limits of violence. A Mexican in *The Cowboy's Baby* (1910) throws the hero's child into a river. The greaser in *A Western Child's Heroism* (1912) attacks the Americans who saved his life. In *Broncho Billy's Redemption* (1910), a vile Mexican is given money to buy medicine for a dying man. Instead he steals the money and tosses away the prescription. *The Greaser's Revenge* (1914) finds José, "the evil halfbreed," trying to kill Fred by throwing him in a deserted mine shaft.

Despite the innate sense of violence among the Mexicans, the greasers had one chance to redeem themselves. Namely, they had to forsake their Mexican brethren, and ally themselves with either the Americans, the landowners, or the business executives when they were threatened by a horde of attacking greasers. In this respect, the "good greaser" becomes the equivalent of the "Uncle Tom" figure that has been seen in films about blacks.

The loyalty is to the master, the dominant race or nation, and never to fellow blacks or Mexicans.

Tony the Greaser (1911) reveals the nature of the "good greaser." The humble Tony loves the landowner's daughter, but as an American she cannot return his affections. A band of "dissolute Mexicans" arrive and threaten both the ranch and the lovely daughter. Tony eventually saves the day, but he is killed in the process. His only reward is to kiss the daughter's handkerchief as he expires. Here is the truly noble greaser! An ad for the film explains that "from force of habit, some might call him a 'Greaser'; true, he is a Mexicano, but a man of noble instincts and chivalrous nature."

The key to the true nature of the Mexican can be found in his relation to North Americans. If the greaser is loyal and brave, he is "good." If he robs and pillages, he becomes an object of scorn.

Whenever Mexicans are placed in conflict with North Americans, the Yankee always wins, owing to his superior moral quality and innate intelligence. The Mexican can never hope to conquer, even if he possesses superior military might, as *The Aztec Treasure* (1914) demonstrates:

Miguel Perez, the Governor of the Province, oppresses and enslaves the peons of Mescalito so that they face starvation. Miguel falls for Dolores, but luckily Miguel's passion is turned momentarily by the capture of Dick Henshaw, a Yankee insurrectionist, who has been leading the insurrectors against the despot. His capture naturally places the revolutionists in a precarious position since they are entirely dependent upon their Yankee leader for success.

Dick easily manages to kill Miguel. He marries Dolores, and discovers the hidden Aztec treasure on their wedding night. He is then "made Governor of the Province and devotes the treasure to the betterment and welfare of the oppressed people."[5]

The Aztec Treasure also reveals two important characteristics of Mexican–American relations in films which have continued to this day. First, Mexicans are often incapable of independent action. Here the revolutionaries are "entirely dependent on their Yankee leader for success." The Mexicans are thus unable to foment a revolution on their own initiative, a "fact" that future events would soon discredit. Second, *The Aztec Treasure* and countless films of the period, reveal the superiority of Yankee love. When given a choice between José or Fred in *The Greaser's Revenge,* the young lady inevitably chooses the North American. While a North American male can marry a high-bred Mexican woman, any Mexican who desires a North American wife is only asking for trouble, as Tony the Greaser discovered.

Despite the blatant stereotypes in these silent films, there was very little criticism in the American press at this time. A review of *Mexican Mine Fraud* (1914) is revealing in this respect:

Much of the action is supposed to have taken place in Mexico, a country with which the average American is a lot more familiar than was the director who made this picture. A sad slip, too, is the introduction of a half-dozen fine looking lions that might have been perfectly at home in South Africa, but fail to convince when introduced apparently as a group captured in Mexico by a band of lion tamers.[6]

Ironically, the critic paid no attention to the comic opera actions of the Mexicans in this film. Only the geographic anachronisms appeared unusual to him. In this fashion, the conventions governing the activities of the Mexican or the greaser were thus well established in the early silent films.

From the Mexican Revolution to World War I

> Pancho Villa tried hard to be a director. He told me to film the funeral of a general. Villa's enemies, the Federal forces, had executed him by lashing him to the tracks and driving a train over him. The funeral spread over three days. I didn't have enough film for half a day. So I cranked the camera without any film in it. It was all I could do. I didn't want to be shot myself.
>
> Charles Rosher in Kevin Brownlow's *The Parade's Gone By*

With the start of the Mexican Revolution, films about the war-torn Republic became more violent than ever. Only now the violence was real as a diverse variety of power contenders competed for control in Mexico City. The difference between motion pictures of revolutions and the actual events began to blur, as one of the leading agrarian revolutionaries, Pancho Villa, signed a contract with the Mutual Film Corporation. For $25,000, the rebel hero allowed Mutual cameramen to follow his exploits. In return, he agreed to fight during daylight hours if possible and try to delay his attacks until the cameras were in position.[7]

Villa agreed to the strange contract since his forces needed money for munitions. Gunther Lessing, a young lawyer, arranged the deal with Villa and deposited the healthy sum in an El Paso bank. Mutual also signed agreements for a second feature, a life of Villa, to be directed by D. W. Griffith. Raoul Walsh was sent to Mexico to shoot background footage and some action scenes. Griffith, however, was too busy filming *The Birth of a Nation,* so the assignment was turned over to Christy Cabanne. The young Walsh portrayed the agrarian hero as a youth in *The Life of Villa* (1915). Villa himself approved the casting.[8]

The Hollywood cameramen who arrived in Mexico finally met the Mexicans whom they had been portraying on the screen. The real life variety of the "greaser" did little to change Hollywood denizens' preconceived notions. Mexico remained a violent and brutal land. Pathé cameraman, Fritz Wagner, relates his experiences:

When I left the City of Mexico for Torreon, I intended to be back in two or three weeks, but since then I have been learning that what a Mexican promises and what he fulfills are two different things. A letter fully detailing my experiences would be 30,000 words long and such a letter is, of course, impossible.

For a couple of days I had nothing to eat and was forced to drink from the mud puddles of the road. The consequence was that when I reached Saltillo, when coming back, I was sick, deadly sick, and became little more than skin and bones. I am not afraid, whatever may happen, but I never thought I would come out alive from this trip.

I have seen four big battles. On each occasion I was threatened with arrest from the Federal general if I took any pictures. He also threatened on one occasion when he caught me turning the crank to smash the camera. He would have done so, too, but for the fact that the rebels came pretty close just then and he had to take it on the run to save his hide.

At Laguna the battle became a rout and the disorganization of the Federal forces was complete. Napoleon's retreat from Moscow was but a disaster on a larger scale. It was every man for himself and the Devil (or the rebels) take the hindmost. I had saved my film and camera (60 lbs.) and went on foot with this load through the desert for 25 miles. I saw my end coming. Nobody would carry my stuff nor could I get a horse at any price. Finally I met a friendly Indian, who brought me to La Hipólita.

For five nights I lay on the stones without a blanket, with my films for a pillow and my camera in my arm. I was afraid to take more than broken naps for fear my camera would be stolen. As it was when I finally got back to Mexico after breaking jail I had left only a shirt, trousers, coat and a pair of shoes. All the rest the rebels got. I tried hard to save my films, but I guess I am lucky at that. Those that I brought with me I had in my pockets. The rest made fine kindling for the campfires of the rebels.

When I arrived in the City of Mexico I got another camera from the Pathé agent there and got busy again. When Huerta heard I was back he sent two secret service men to the hotel, who confiscated all my papers and films. They did leave the camera. From then on I had the unpleasant experience of seeing myself constantly shadowed. Any time I would open the door of my room there would be a murderous-looking individual standing near by. At the dining table would be another, who would scarce take his eyes from me. I became so nervous that the running of a mouse across the room at night would make me jump up in the bed in a cold sweat. I expected every moment to either be thrown into some dungeon or else knifed in the back. A man can stand an out and out fight—it is the deadly danger constantly impending that wears a man out.

Finally one day Huerta sent for me and told me to develop the films (under supervision) and project them for him. He censored the films, had me cut out all the parts unfavorable to the Federals and then ordered the "Salon Rojo" show them as advertising for his troops. Huerta was much pleased with his show, otherwise I would have lost the films. I saw my chance and decided to beat it before another storm broke. I told the Chief of Police that Huerta had O.K.'d the films and that it was all right for me to go to Vera Cruz. The Chief was very decent and gave me his card, which I used as a passport. I hid myself in a freight car and finally got to Vera Cruz O.K.

When Victor Miller, your cameraman, arrived with a new outfit for me, for the first time in weeks I was able to eat with an appetite and sleep as a man should sleep."[9]

Considerable hoopla surrounded the first showings of *Barbarous Mexico,* also known as *War in Mexico,* in 1913. Before the premiere, Mutual offered the rights to the considerable footage it had acquired:

To the victor belong the spoils and if you want to share in the fruits of Villa's conquests get control of the . . . right to exhibit . . . war pictures made by the Mutual Film Corporation under special contract with Villa himself! Villa is getting more famous every day. There is three times more about him in the newspapers than about any other man alive. . . . The picture introduces hundreds of scenes taken during the Battles of Torreón, Chihuahua, and other famous conflicts and other scenes showing the tragic early life and adventures of the wonderful warrior, the greatest military genius since Napoleon.[10]

The resulting films were as violent as the advertisements proclaimed. The *New York Times* praised the film at its premiere, noting that "there are many scenes in which General Villa is seen directing the movement of his troops and artillery, and cavalry battles are shown with remarkable clearness. Other views show the burning of dead bodies on the battlefield."[11]

During the Revolutionary period, Hollywood received its first inkling that Latins might not appreciate their standard film image. This incident occurred in Monclova, Mexico, where Solax features was filming a conventional Western. Two of the Mexican extras became enraged because the story called for their capture by the American heroes. As a result, they changed the script and fired their guns at the Americans. Fortunately, the guns contained blank cartridges, but the affair started a fight between the American crew and the Mexicans. Soldiers were called in to quell the fighting, and the culprits were flogged with the flat side of a sword.[12]

World War I did far more to end the derogatory portrayals on the American screen than did any isolated incidents or complaints from South American governments. A variety of notions caused this abrupt change which led to the virtual elimination of the word greaser in films appearing after 1917. First of all, there was a shift of villains. Now, the Kaiser and the Hun were the enemy, not the Mexican next door.

Second, the European war made the export of French or British films to Latin America much more difficult. For the first time, Hollywood had an opportunity to make commercial inroads in a vast territory it had formerly ignored. Arthur T. Lang, export manager of the Nicholas Power Company, explained that the time was ripe for Hollywood: "But now, an entirely new situation—as remarkable as it was unexpected—has arisen, opening the way to the rapid development of export trade in American films and providing an opportunity not merely for the pioneers, but for all the film manufacturers of the country to cash in heavily."[13]

If Hollywood hoped to expand its markets during this period, derogatory views of the Latin had to be shunned. As a result, the greaser almost disappeared from the screen. Unfortunately, the Latin was not replaced, for the time being, by a new Mexican, who was intelligent, cultured, and refined. The only way that Hollywood could deal with its stock character was not to change it but to eliminate it.

The film industry cultivated its new market with a passion, after certain cultural misunderstandings had been alleviated. The first major problem was the language barrier. Film distributors insisted on using English in their catalogues and correspondence. F. C. Roberts, of the San Juan, Puerto Rico, Bureau of Labor, wrote a letter to *Moving Picture World* explaining the difficulties that might arise from this practice: "In Latin America there is not even one for every three thousand that speaks English. They only speak Spanish or Portuguese and these are the languages they use exclusively for everything. Therefore, when these people receive a catalogue printed in English, it produces the same effect as if the American people were to receive catalogues in Chinese."[14]

A few months after this complaint appeared, *Motion Picture World* established a Spanish edition, *Cine-Mundial,* to facilitate the film distribution process in South America. The advertisements for the new trade magazine proclaimed that it "is edited by natives of Spanish speaking countries. These men have a wide and intimate knowledge of conditions in our Latin sister-Republics. *They speak the real language of these countries,* not a poor imitation!"[15]

At virtually the same time, a new process of subtitling was developed. Rather than provide each print with Spanish-language subtitles, each nation prepared its own subtitles for the American films. These were then printed and projected alongside the English titles by the use of a separate projector. Once the showings were completed, the films could then be returned unchanged to the American distributor.[16]

The result of this active catering to South American markets led to a marked increase in the number of American films shown. One foreign visitor to Rio de Janeiro in 1916 complained that "it took a considerable search to find anything but American-made films."[17] Yet, although Hollywood showed a marked economic interest in South America, there was no attempt to woo this new audience with films about their own native land. Latins viewed the same films American audiences saw during this time period. Such films as *Tillie's Tomato Surprise, The Riddle of the Silk Stocking, The Right Girl,* and *In the Shadows of the Pyramids* were among the most popular films in Argentina in 1916.[18] American distributors viewed this interest in North America as quite natural: "Just as our people like to see films representing conditions in far-away lands, so are Latin audiences interested in films showing American life, institutions, humor and scenery. They like our clean-cut romances and they enjoy films with a strong touch of industrialism, especially if it borders on the spectacular, and they are keen for our western pictures."[19]

During the wartime period there were few attacks on film producers for presenting Latins in an unfavorable light. This owed primarily to the disappearance of the Mexican villain on the screen and the substitution of the treacherous Hun. Indicative of the calm in the relationship between the Latin countries and the motion picture producers was the placid session at the Pan-American Conference in Buenos Aires. Normally these meetings are hectic affairs which allow the South American

nations to vent their wrath on American policy. Here, only financial matters were discussed with film distributors in such sessions
as "The Necessity of Better Transportation Facilities in the
American Republics," "Improved Banking Facilities," and "The
Copyright Situation." No one mentioned the Latin image in film,
an issue that had disturbed international conferences earlier in
the century.[20]

Thus, while Hollywood achieved what was primarily an economic goal, both government officials and newspapers praised
the film makers' goodwill in these troubled times: "The closer
union of the two Americas is one of the gratifying things that is
coming out of the great war cloud whose silver lining has so long
been hidden. It is hoped that the Western Hemisphere will never
be subjected to the hatreds and misunderstandings that have
wrought such destruction in the Eastern. Men of vision in all the
countries concerned should work toward harmony both now and
in the future."[21]

The wartime rhetoric seemed to portend a glowing period in
inter-American relations. The greaser had apparently vanished
and Hollywood might continue its enterprise of goodwill. However, with the ending of the war, the bubble burst and disrep-
utable Latins returned once again to the American screen.

Whither the Greaser?   1919–1928

> At the present time there is a picture in one of
> the leading Broadway theatres purporting to
> have a "Brazilian" mien. One of the characters
> has the name Alvadorez. This is not a Brazilian
> name, and I believe it was taken from some
> make of cigar.
>
> Letter to the editor
> *New York Times*, March 17, 1925

The fragile façade of inter-American unity was shattered after
the war, and previous stereotypes returned to the American
screen. An advertisement for the film *Rio Grande* (1919) made it
appear as though the interregnum of the war years had never

occurred: "Take the hot blood of Mexico and mix it fifty-fifty with the cooler, calmer strain of the Northern neighbor and what happens? You can gamble on it that the daughter of the union will blow hot, blow cold, . . . that she will be passionate, revengeful, brave, unreasonable, and most cussedly loveable."

Rex Beach, the novelist, explorer, and motion picture producer, also turned his attention to the lands south of the border, and claimed to discover an isle of cannibals, "A savage people who know scarcely anything of the great world revolving around them, and, astonishingly, still cling to the practice of eating their own kind." He dismissed Mexico as "an unkempt land, rather careless of its civilization," and noted that "it is not an unusual thing to travel with an armored car both fore and aft."[22]

By this time, Mexico had had enough. It was no longer going to be ridiculed on the screens of the world. In late 1919, the Mexican government sent a formal letter to film producers protesting their emphasis on "films of squalor." The pronouncement explained that "these films do not portray the average conditions in the country." Rather, the government contended that "photographers travel about, seeking the worst conditions they can find, and compose their films entirely of such pictures." The letter ended with a subtle warning, as the government threatened to restrict motion picture photography in Mexico.

This informal warning did little to change Hollywood practices, as *Rio Grande* and the Rex Beach episode reveal. By February, 1922, the Mexican government decided to ban all films that portrayed Mexicans unfavorably. By itself, this action would have done little to restrict Hollywood productions which cast Mexicans as villains. The offending film could still be distributed to other countries and little profit would be lost. As a result, the Mexican government decided to ban *all films* produced by the company that produced the offensive film. This was quite a strong ultimatum to be delivered at the height of the American film industry's expansion southward. The Famous Players–Lasky offices, which had just completed a one-hundred-film deal with Mexican distributors, was shaken by the pronouncement and issued a statement saying that "the wishes of the government would be respected."

The reason for this action was obvious. A high official of the Mexican government explained that "the usual portrayal of the Mexican in moving pictures is as a bandit or a sneak. Ill will toward Mexico has been inflamed by these pictures to such an extent, that the Mexican government found it necessary to make such a protest."[23]

Mexico was not alone in its ban of film companies that offended national sentiments. Panama followed soon after with similar legislation, after the filming on its soil of Ne'er Do-Well (1923). Bad vibrations began soon after the cast and crew arrived. Lila Lee, the female star, was quoted as saying that she "had lived largely on iguanas while in Panama," a remark quite far from the truth.[24] She was forced to apologize publicly so the film company would not be expelled. The film itself also offended Panamanian audiences, since once again Latin society was portrayed as primitive and the Latin lover loses the woman to a North American.

The Ne'er Do-Well is Kirk Anthony (Thomas Meighan), the idle son of a millionaire. He has only two interests — women and wine. One night, after sipping a little too much of the spirits, Kirk's rich friends deposit him on a freighter bound for Panama. He arrives at the Canal without a cent. His only possession is a white shirt with the phone numbers of his girl friends written on the back. He immediately falls in love with Chiquita (Lila Lee), the daughter of a Panamanian politician. Kirk easily steals Chiquita from her current beau, Ramon Alfarez (Sid Smith), a diminutive police inspector. Ramon hasn't a chance once Chiquita spots the North American. He becomes jealous, but it is to no avail. Kirk marries Chiquita and returns to his father's estate. Once again, the so-called Latin Lover is found lacking.[25]

The Panamanian legislation surpassed that of the Mexican in severity. Article seven of the legislation proclaimed that "the filming and exhibition of films tending to discredit or lower the prestige of the country, or which may in any form involve propaganda prejudicial to the moral, social, and economic interests of the nation are prohibited." Films were not alone in this vast censorship based on questions of prestige. Reporters might be expelled for "transmitting prejudicial news." Even the makers of postal cards had to beware. Anyone who produced photographs which "discredit the race or misrepresent national customs" would be fined heavily.[26]

What was Hollywood to do? How could it replace its most popular and most thoroughly vile villain. A French, Dutch, or Italian substitution would merely offend European audiences. The solution lay in the abandoning of Mexican and Central American locales and in switching scenes to the Argentine several thousand miles away. The result of the Mexican restrictions was merely to move the standard Latin American stereotypes to a new location. Thus, the domination of Mexican locales in Hollywood films vanished in the 1920s as producers sought to avoid the troublesome restrictions. The Latin's new homes were now Brazil and Argentina, areas that had been rarely considered in the first two decades of the century.

One of the first films of this scenic shift, *Argentine Love* (1924), featured Ricardo Cortez and Bebe Daniels, in a standard Latin-styled love story. Bebe Daniels, portraying an Argentine, falls in love with a North American stranger. This angers Ricardo, a "hot-blooded Argentinian," and he vows to murder anyone who looks at Bebe. Bebe pretends to love Ricardo so he will not harm her true love. As Ricardo is about to attack Bebe, he is suddenly shot. All ends happily, and the lovers are reunited. The film was reputedly so trite and poorly acted, that a critic for the *New York Times* commented: "In the end the American and heroine are so glad that it is all over that they give a blasé glance at the bullet ridden body of the hot-headed man." He could imagine the director saying at the finale, "Get ready with the tears when I clap my hands. Look as Spanish as you can—all except the hero!"[27]

The Gaucho (1927) arrived on the screen shortly thereafter, and it offered little improvement in the stock portrayal of Latin Americans, whether Mexican or Argentine. At first it seemed that this film might display technical accuracy. Douglas Fairbanks, the star of the film, insisted on learning to use the bola, the weapon of the *gauchos,* with consummate proficiency. Fairbanks insisted that Argentine experts, Nick Milanesio and Andrés Rodríguez, be flown to Hollywood for several months. Fairbanks later claimed that it took him longer to use the bolas than to make the film. Not only did Fairbanks have to learn to use the bola, but his two hundred cohorts in the film had to master the weapon. Ironically, Fairbanks's sidekicks were mostly Mexican. Therefore, as one expert explained, "the bola was as unfamiliar to them as croquet to an American Indian or baseball to an Eskimo."[28] Thus, the Mexicans were once again bandits, even though the film proclaimed them Argentine gauchos.

Once the crew of two hundred and one "gauchos" learned to use the bolas, all attempts at technical accuracy were stopped. The story itself bore no relation to the Argentine, or anywhere else in South America. Fairbanks admitted that he conceived the idea for the story while visiting Our Lady of Lourdes in France! *The Gaucho* concerns a victim of the "black doom" (leprosy). Fairbanks antagonizes a leper at a fiesta when he proclaims that "anyone suffering from the disease ought to go forth and put an end to himself." The gaucho's sentiments are put to the test when he, too, contracts the disease after a struggle with Lupe Velez, who is a Mexican portraying an Argentine. The Madonna appears and tells the gaucho to visit her holy shrine. Fairbanks follows her bidding and is eventually cured of leprosy.

When the Argentine solution appeared impractical to producers desirous of using stock Latin villains, another alternative arose. Rather than use the name of an actual country and risk offending its inhabitants, screenwriters began to create mythical cities and nations. *The Dove* (1928), directed by Roland West, provides the most notorious example. The film concerns Don José María y Sandoval (Noah Beery), who considers himself "the bes' dam *caballero* in Costa Roja." Costa Roja, as the title cards explain, is located in the Mediterranean!

This unsubtle guise fooled hardly anyone. Mordaunt Hall, critic for the *New York Times,* explained: "Taken by and large, José is perhaps a screen character to which the Mexican government might have objected, for he is greedy, sensuous, boastful, cold-blooded, irritable, and quite a wine-bibber, but he does dress well. . . . He hates to have his luncheon spoiled by a noisy victim of his shooting squad. He adores beauty, but he is inconstant."[29] Thus, the Costa Roja subterfuge diffuses any possible criticism since José is not a resident of any present-day Latin American country. Unfortunately, when *The Dove* was remade during the sound era as *Girl of the Rio* (1932), the screenwriters apparently forgot this distinction and situated this film in a Mexican bordertown. As a result Mexico renewed its long-standing threat to ban motion picture companies that produced films offensive to Mexicans.

Thus, little had changed in the first three decades of films concerning Latin America. The Mexican remained the same unruly bandit whether on his native soil or in Brazil or Argentina. Hollywood remained smug in its indifference. As the era of the sound film dawned, South Americans and Hollywood producers remained as far apart as ever. A confrontation at a dinner for motion picture advertisers in 1927 in New York City revealed the depth of these differences. Herbert Hoover, then Secretary of Commerce, and James J. Walker, Mayor of New York City, attended the affair. The guests of honor were the ambassadors of the Central and South American nations.

Hoover came to the podium and welcomed his distinguished guests. He praised the motion picture industry to the skies:

I trust in the good faith of this great body of men who dominate the industry in the United States to carry out this profound obligation—that is, that every picture of South American life shown to our people and every picture of North American life shown to the South American people should carry those ideals which build for that respect and confidence which is the real guarantee of peace and progress.

He added that the industry must censor itself, for at no time would he sanction government intervention in the choice of film topics or their treatment.

The South Americans in the audience were not fooled by Hoover's words. The Chilean ambassador, Miguel Cruchaga Tocornal, responded for the group, expressing the opinions of Latin Americans on the matter. Cruchaga's reply indicated that he was familiar with virtually every Latin stereotype yet seen on the American screen.

The myth of Spanish-American lovers serenading their fair ladies under iron-grilled balconies bathed by romantic moonlight and alive with the beauty of red carnations; and the injustice of portraying all those who hail from south of the Rio Grande as born villains to be conquered by the mighty, iron-fisted, two-gunned vigilante; and the perpetuation of such absurdities as picturing an Argentine gentleman on his wedding day in the brilliant dress of a bullfighter, when the colorful Spanish entertainment is forbidden in that progressive country—these are things that we call, with a friendly smile of forebearance, Hollywoodisms.[30]

Shortly thereafter, the stereotypes of the silent era would appear ridiculously simple. With the advent of sound, new and more complex versions of Latin life and society could be presented on the screen. Unfortunately, there was little improvement. As Lupe Velez later commented, "eet stinks!"

THE FILMS AND THE STARS

Ramon Novarro and the Myth of the Latin Lover

> It is hard to write about one of these outstanding, whole-wheat boys. My sympathies are all with the criminal classes. And Ramon is not one of these, even though he is a Hollywood resident and a Mexican.
>
> Not that I mean any disparagement of Mexicans.
>
> Herbert Howe
> Photoplay, April, 1923

Women must be wooed long and ardently,
preferably under balconies.

Ramon Novarro
Photoplay, April, 1923

The legend of the Latin Lover has so beclouded the image of
the Latin American on the screen that it is difficult to discuss the
subject without passion. The sensual sighs evoked by Rudolph
Valentino or Ramon Novarro offer a marked contrast with the
laughter or disdain provoked by *Tony the Greaser* or *The Aztec
Treasure*. The Latin Lover is the most sensual male on the screen,
yet the majority of films about Latin Americans reveal an effete
asexual comedic figure, who always loses the heroine when she
meets a Yankee stranger.

Part of the confusion stems from the use of the term "Latin."
Only rarely was it synonymous with "Latin American." More
often than not, the Latin Lover was of Italian descent, as this
review of *Latin Blood* reveals: "Gains, an Italian gardener, is an
employee on the estate of the rich and beautiful Lucia. His
emotional nature makes him fall madly in love with the mistress,
but his dull brain prevents his realizing how ridiculous it is."[31]

The concept of the Latin Lover was indicative more of a
character type epitomized by Rudolph Valentino than of a geographical region. The swarthy complexion, the narrow lips, the
dark hair, and the passionate eyes became the trademarks of the
Latin Lover. Only rarely did the Latin Lover coincide with a Latin
American. Ramon Novarro was one of the few exceptions.

Ramon Novarro was a rarity, a Latin Lover who was also a
Latin American. He was one of thirteen children, born in Durango, Mexico, in 1899. The young José Ramón Gil Samaniegos
traced his heritage to both Spanish and Aztec nobility: "The
imperial blood of the Aztecs flows through the heart of Novarro,
and he takes pride in a lineage pointing back four hundred years
to the opulent court of Montezuma, where Cortes stood amazed
by splendor, in a palace of three hundred rooms, the walls of

alabaster hung in tapestries of feathers and the floors of mosaic, like carpets made of jewels."[32]

As a youth in Mexico City, Novarro became an ardent movie fan, and at age seventeen he left for Hollywood with dreams of becoming a star. In the interim, he became a professional tango dancer with his youngest sister Carmen. After countless performances as an extra in silent films, Rex Ingram picked the youth for a secondary role in The Prisoner of Zenda (1922).

His third film for Ingram, Where the Pavement Ends (1923), established him as a star. Yet, this motion picture reveals the sense of ambiguity that trailed an incipient Latin Lover who was also a Latin American. Although part of the film was shot in Cuba, it is essentially the story of a South Sea pagan chief who falls in love with a missionary's daughter. Miss Matilda (Alice Terry) meets Motauri (Novarro) in front of a passion vine. They vow undying love, but the dissolute Captain Gregson spots them and reports the incident to the girl's father. In the meantime, Gregson resolves to stop selling firewater to the islanders in order to pass into the missionary's good graces, and, consequently, marry his daughter. Matilda is repulsed by this idea, so she attempts to elope with Motauri. Unfortunately, the cagey Gregson has removed all the boats from the island. The chief is forced to return to his tribe to get a new boat. In the meantime, Matilda realizes that her husband-to-be, although not so dark-complected, is the chief of a tribe of blacks. She then tells Motauri that she cannot marry him. The chief, true to his tribal traditions, jumps to his death in a ravine.

This ending was somewhat depressing to the exhibitors who viewed the release print which featured the new Latin Lover of the screen. They implored Ingram to shoot a second ending.[33] The new denouement allows Motauri to discover that he is really of Caucasian parentage, and, consequently, he may marry Miss Matilda. Although Novarro was masquerading as an islander, the film revealed the essential ambiguity of this Latin Lover. As a Caucasian he was free to marry the missionary's daughter. As a member of a colored minority, whether black, Polynesian, or

Latin American, such a marriage was impossible. Here, the pagan was no different than poor *Tony the Greaser.*

Despite Novarro's rapid rise to fame, he rarely portrayed a Latin American in any of his films. As a result, American audiences would be hard-pressed to identify the Latin Lover with the Latin American despite superficial similarities in facial characteristics. An interview in *Photoplay* revealed Novarro's multinational identity on the screen: "In point of fact he is a cosmopolite. Probably no star has traveled the earth so extensively as Novarro, in his brief career, or played characters of so many nationalities. The Austrian Rupert of *The Prisoner of Zenda* marked his debut. Then followed that pagan Polynesian of the South Seas in *Where the Pavement Ends;* the French hero of *Scaramouche* (1923); the Spaniard of *Thy Name Is Woman* (1924); the Arab dragoman in *The Arab* (1924); prince of Jerusalem in the Lew Wallace classic *Ben Hur* (1926); and now—at last—an American in *The Midshipman* (1925), produced at the U.S. Naval Academy."[34]

"At last—an American." These very words reveal a hint of resentment of Novarro's Latin American background in the early days of his career. On one occasion, Novarro protested a publicity release which described him as Spanish. He then "insisted on the truth of his American birth." An interviewer also noted: "Against this romantic background of Aztec splendor, Novarro has suffered the appellation of "Latin" in silence. It was characteristic of the Aztecs to support any pain with stoicism. As the facts stand, he is more genuinely American than the descendants of those who suffered mal de mer on the Mayflower; their ancestors compared to his are *nouveau.*"[35]

As a result of the diversity of Novarro's film roles, the concept of the Latin Lover remained definitively separated from the Latin American. Although Novarro was of Mexican descent, his filmic persona betrayed no trace of the film image of the Mexican so common in the silent era. As a result, the Latin Lover remained the property of Mediterranean civilization rather than of South America. Not until the arrival of Fernando Lamas and Ricardo

Montalban in Hollywood during the late 1940s and early 1950s would the concept of the Latin Lover become the province of Spanish Americans.

Douglas Fairbanks as *The Americano*

The Latin American always suffered by comparison with the Yankee during the silent era. Whenever a Yankee arrived on the scene, the Latin became either more stupid or more despicable. These films approached imperialistic epics, as the North American hero became all-powerful, all-knowing, and the most sensual man on the screen.

One of Anita Loos's early screenplays featured Douglas Fairbanks as the Great White Hope of the chaotic Latin country of Paragonia. The name of this mythical nation provided the first clue to the nature of the stereotypes that would be present on the screen in *The Americano* (1916). Whenever Latin Americans were portrayed as despicable, a false name that sounded South American was chosen for the nation by Hollywood screenwriters in order to avoid the official protests of the country from south of the border.

Douglas Fairbanks portrays a foremost American mining engineer. The country of Paragonia sends a representative to Fairbanks's firm to seek aid for the troubled mining industry. Worker agitation has caused the mines to be sabotaged. Unemployment is rampant, and revolution threatens. Fairbanks at first refuses the pleas of the Paragonian minister, but then he reconsiders once he meets with President Valdes and his beautiful daughter Juana (Alma Rubens). Valdes claims that he is helpless: "Without American capital and engineers our mines are useless." Juana winks at Fairbanks, and he decides to help the beleaguered president.

As Fairbanks arrives in Paragonia, he discovers that Valdes has been overthrown by the Generals García and Sánchez in a bloody military coup. García is less receptive to the American interests and calls the Yankees "pigs." At this point, Fairbanks decides to enter the revolution on the side of the deposed Valdes. Prime Minister Castille, disguised as a beggar, contacts Fairbanks and takes him to the incarcerated president.

As the American mining engineer is plotting the escape of Valdes, he is summoned by the Generals Sánchez and García. Like Valdes, they are unable to reopen the mines, and as a result, they fear counterrevolution. Fairbanks is unreceptive to the pleas of the dictators. Unlike Valdes and his daughter, these vile usurpers are of *mestizo* stock, with dark hair and skin, and huge black moustaches. They lack the refined and genteel air of the Caucasian Valdes family, which is obviously of Spanish heritage. Consequently, Fairbanks pretends to cooperate, but continues his attempts to free the captured Valdes.

The citizenry of Paragonia are driven to revolt, but they accomplish nothing. Only with Fairbanks's aid does the counterrevolution succeed. First he frees the jailed president. Then he single-handedly enters the office of the dictators and beats them to a pulp. It is Fairbanks who greets the cheering masses from the presidential palace balcony: "I am here to assure you that the mines will be opened and that the nation will be governed honestly." He returns power to President Valdes, and then he marries Juana. As the ultimate reward for his aid, Fairbanks is made the commander in chief of the Paragonian armed forces as the film ends.

This film embraces the theme of the powerless Latin American. Only the American mining engineer is able to put the country right, by restoring "stability" and reopening the mines. Once he has accomplished his task, he retains the effective control of the government. Indeed, Fairbanks seems symbolic of the United States government interventions in Puerto Rico, Cuba, and Santo Domingo at the beginning of the century. Fairbanks becomes the imperialist par excellence, and Latin Americans have little or no control of the affairs of their own political system. Thus, as the silent era ends, the Latin on the screen remains abject, powerless, corrupt, and pathetic. Matters seemingly could only improve as the advent of sound revolutionizes the film industry. Will the image of the Latin be improved as well?

NOTES

1. Terry Ramsaye, *A Million and One Nights: A History of the Motion Picture* (New York, 1964), pp. 282–284.

2. Ibid., pp. 290–291.

3. Ibid., p. 839.

4. *Moving Picture World,* 22 (October, 1914), 469.

5. Ibid., 22 (September 23, 1914), 1686.

6. Ibid., 21 (July, 1914), 84.

7. Kevin Brownlow, *The Parade's Gone By* (New York, 1968), p. 224.

8. Ibid.

9. *Moving Picture World,* 21 (July 18, 1914), 440.

10. Ibid., 22 (July 11, 1914), 341.

11. *New York Times (NYT),* May 10, 1914.

12. *Moving Picture World,* 21 (July, 1914), 80.

13. Ibid., 22 (October, 1914), 467.

14. Ibid., 27 (March 18, 1916), 1812.

15. Ibid., 28 (April 22, 1916), 84.

16. Ibid., 34 (December 22, 1917), 1796.

17. Ibid., 32 (May 5, 1917), 789, 955.

18. Ibid., 27 (March 25, 1916), 1983.

19. Ibid., 22 (October 1, 1914), 467.

20. Ibid., 27 (March 25, 1916), 1983.

21. Ibid., 36 (May 20, 1918), 1546. See also: *New York Evening Sun,* May 20, 1918.

22. Ibid., 40 (April 26, 1919), 532.

23. *NYT,* February 11, 1922.

24. Ibid., September 19, 1926.

25. Ibid., May 1, 1923.

26. Ibid., September 19, 1926.

27. Ibid., December 28, 1924.

28. Ibid., October 16, 1927.

29. Ibid., January 3, 1928.

30. Ibid., April 3, 1927.

31. *Moving Picture World,* 21 (August, 1914), 861.

32. *Photoplay,* 28 (October, 1925), 46.

33. DeWitt Bodeen, "Ramon Novarro," *Films in Review,* 18 (November, 1967), 532.

34. *Photoplay,* 28 (October, 1925), 46.

35. Ibid.

3

FROM BANDIT
TO PRESIDENT

LATIN IMAGES IN AMERICAN FILMS
1928-1939

The image of the Mexican as a rapacious bandit almost disappeared from American screens by the end of the 1920s. When official complaints to American film producers and the United States government appeared futile, the Mexican government clamped an embargo on all films which presented Latins in a derogatory manner. Thus, films like *Tony the Greaser* (1911) or *The Greaser's Gauntlet* (1908), which had been common earlier in the century, were swiftly eliminated from production schedules.[1] By 1928, Mexico and her Latin neighbors became relatively satisfied with the elimination of these unfavorable stereotypes of South Americans. Hollywood, however, appeared at a loss, as though unable to depict a Mexican in any other occupation than bandit or lazy peasant. As a result, films with Latin themes or settings slowly faded from the screens.

The advent of sound films abruptly changed this situation, bringing new problems as well as confounding old ones. Latin American audiences generally favored the new "talkies" and often greeted them rapturously. In Rio de Janeiro, perhaps the South American city most responsive to foreign trends, audiences flocked to see *Broadway Melody* (MGM, 1929), which grossed more than any other film yet presented in Brazil. The sales of English-language phonograph records increased considerably with the arrival of the American sound film, and one critic noted that people would repeat dialogue from the film when conversing with friends in order to practice the language. Gilberto Souto, critic of *Frou-Frou,* predicted that "every Brazilian would be speaking English perfectly within two years due to the coming of talkies which are taking the country by storm."[2]

The initial responsiveness to American sound films soon cooled after some cautious reflection. By 1931, the new films gradually came to be seen as "invaders destroying the purity of the Spanish language." Some politicians even warned that the Spanish language might disappear. Thus, the disfavor with American films shifted to a linguistic question and the problem of offensive Latin stereotypes was forgotten in the face of this more urgent threat. The Argentine daily *La Prensa* warned against the "spiritual conquest" of the American sound film, which was "rapidly undermining national social standards."[3] As a result, the municipal councils of Medellín, Colombia, Puebla, Mexico, and São Paulo, Brazil, proposed heavy taxes on all American sound films shown in their districts. Alexandre Albuquerque, of the São Paulo council, voiced this sentiment when he urged a $60 fine on each foreign language film shown in Brazil, since "they were unpatriotic and prejudicial to the Portuguese tongue."[4]

In addition to the linguistic threat posed by the growing number of English films released in South America, Latins also faced an influx of American-produced Spanish-language films. With the coming of sound, Hollywood executives realized the possible loss of a considerable part of the Spanish American market since subtitles could not be used when a great portion of the moviegoing audience was illiterate. This assumption of general illiteracy proved so pervasive that the Olympia Theater of Bogotá constructed a screen along the center of the theater. The rich, and presumably those who could read, purchased expensive seats *in front of* the screen so that they might view the subtitles comfortably. The poor, however, could only purchase seats *behind* the screen, where the subtitles appeared in reverse.[5] This apparently caused no problem since it was assumed that this portion of the audience was unable to read anyway. It was this sector of the theatergoing audience that Hollywood was trying to capture by the production of over seventy Spanish-language films between 1930 and 1936.[6]

Ironically, although the films were aimed at Spanish-speaking audiences, they committed countless linguistic blunders which both infuriated and amused Latin audiences. First, these films were consistently cheap productions. Often, they would be shot at night, with a Spanish-speaking director and cast performing on the set of an English-language film being produced during the day. In this manner a Spanish version of *Dracula* (1931) was shot almost concurrently with the Bela Lugosi version. The results of these early efforts were consistently embarrassing to South American audiences. Hollywood executives, in their hurry to capture the Spanish market, gathered every Spanish-speaking actor at hand to perform in these films. Unfortunately, Spanish is not a uniform language since it is subject to strong regional variations. As a result, Cubans performed with Argentines, Chileans, Mexicans, and peninsular Spaniards. The ultimate results of this linguistic potpourri appeared ludicrous to Latin audiences. Americans might experience a similar reaction to a film version of *Hamlet* performed by a Southern colonel, a New England dowager, a Texas cowboy, and a Brooklyn taxi driver.

In response to early criticism of these films, producers adopted a policy of using actors who spoke Castilian Spanish. This variety of Spanish is spoken mainly on the Spanish peninsula and tends to pronounce the *z* and the soft *c* like the English *th*. The bitter irony of this capricious decision lay in the fact that 90 percent of the audience for these Spanish-language films would be Latin Americans who did not speak Castilian Spanish. This move infuriated both Latin audiences and South Americans living in the United States. In Los Angeles a Friends of Latin America Club produced a journal *Cine Parlante Español* (Spanish Language Cinema) which argued that "the self-imposed purists of the Spanish language in Hollywood" should change their decision and gear their movies to Latin American audiences.[7]

Hollywood's manner of producing Spanish-language films revealed a basic assumption which governed all relations with the South American countries. Hollywood believed that Latin America was a uniform entity, unaffected by cultural, geographical, or social differences. Thus, despite the importance of the South American market, Hollywood paid little attention to the linguistic differences within the continent, and as a result doomed its cinematic domination of the region to failure. Ironically, the absurdity of these American productions actually encouraged the development of local product in Argentina, Mexico, and Brazil, which competed admirably with the American-produced films.[8]

The assumption of cultural uniformity gradually gave rise to the question of Latin images in American films, an issue that had lain dormant in recent years owing to the dilemmas arising with the arrival of the new sound films. By 1933, the reemergence of old stereotypes began to be perceived, although in a less blatant form than formerly. All of Latin America was still depicted as a cultural backwater, populated by evil bandits and dancing maidens. Again, government embargoes and official censorship was brought into action in the face of an influx of American films which insulted the integrity of the Latin countries.

The Brazilian government first asked that the film *Rio's Road to Hell* (1931) be suppressed, but the State Department dismissed the request arguing that "it could find no precedent governing the situation."[9] The Motion Picture Exhibitor's Union followed suit in Havana, Cuba, where it vowed that no MGM film would be shown until *Cuban Love Song* (1931) was withdrawn from the market. The Cuban Secretary of the Interior explained that he had received countless complaints which argued that this Jeanette MacDonald–Lawrence Tibbett film "depicted the island as an uncivilized country where the natives are half-clothed and barefoot, and the local magistrates impose absurd penalties on foreigners."[10]

These complaints were swiftly solved and emerged as minor issues compared with the furor resulting from the release of RKO's *Girl of the Rio,* directed by Herbert Brenon in 1932. The theater that showed the film in Mexico City received constant threats of violence, and a special delegation visited President Ortiz Rubio to request immediate suspension of the film. The bitter resentment over *Girl of the Rio* can be easily understood, since the film featured two prominent stars of Mexican heritage, Dolores Del Rio[11] and Leo Carrillo,[12] in unflattering roles. From the first moment that Carrillo enters the Purple Pigeon Night Club to strains from *Carmen,* he appears as one of the most vile Mexicans yet portrayed on the screen. As the oil-rich Señor Tostado (toast), Carrillo is interested only in drink, money, sex, and violence. He resolves to marry Del Rio, but she is in love with Johnny Powell, an American. Carrillo frames Johnny in a murder case and then agrees to spare his life if Del Rio will come away with him. Despite such corruption, Señor Tostado continually comments that "he is the best *caballero* in all Mexico." If this is indeed the "best *caballero* in all Mexico," then the Mexican chargé d'affaires in Washington had a justifiable complaint when he requested that the film be banned.[13]

The anger with *Girl of the Rio* spread beyond Mexican borders, with Panama and Nicaragua agreeing to prohibit showings of the film.[14] This unofficial cooperation gradually gave rise to a series of reciprocal treaties in the face of continual insults to Latin audiences. The importance of this issue was revealed by the numerous discussions of the matter at the Inter-American Conference at Buenos Aires in 1936. The model for a series of agreements on this matter became the Film Treaty between Spain and San Salvador negotiated in 1935. The countries agreed to

regard as disparaging to and to prohibit the trade and circulation and exhibition in both countries of cinematographic films or reels, sound or silent, produced by any process whatsoever, which attack, slander, defame, or ridicule, insult, or misrepresent directly or indirectly, the uses, institutions, habits, characteristics, or peculiarities of or incidents occurring in Spain and Salvador.[15]

Additionally, they agreed that repeated offenses would warrant an embargo of all future films produced by the offending companies.

Spain also concluded similar agreements with Nicaragua, Peru, and Chile in 1935 and 1936. Peru also signed treaties with Chile and Argentina in the same period. Each country agreed to prohibit films offensive to the other contracting party.[16]

The most common reason for prohibiting a film or deleting certain scenes remained the derogatory portrayal of a national citizen. Columbia's *Lawless Rider* (1937) was thus banned "because a character depicted as a Mexican, wearing a big sombrero, is kicked around and laughed at." In the Jeanette MacDonald and Nelson Eddy musical, *Girl of the Golden West* (MGM, 1930), all scenes depicting Mexicans as bandits were eliminated, which reportedly left only a fraction of the original print for exhibition.

Any film that depicted a national hero in an unfavorable light also saw the censor's shears. In order to avoid such postproduction censorship, MGM entered into negotiations with the Mexican government in order to produce an acceptable *Viva Villa!* in 1934. Although the government approved a final script which toned down the Don Juan nature of the revolutionary hero, both the press and the public were offended by the comic overtones in Wallace Beery's portrayal of Villa. Additionally, the film's cast showed little respect for Mexicans who assisted in the making of the film. Lee Tracy insulted the Mexican Military Academy cadets by urinating from the balcony of the St. Regis Hotel, and, in order to avoid an international incident, he was swiftly fired and replaced by the more docile Stu Erwin. Beery also insulted the small pueblo where the film was shot: rather than accept the town's hospitality, he flew back to Mexico City every night for his hotel accommodations. The film received a chilly reception when it finally premiered in Mexico City as vandals threw firecrackers into the crowded theater and wounded three women. The government then banned the film until tensions eased.[17] From this date even the slightest mention of Villa in North American films was looked on with disdain. As a result, *Motor Madness* (1937) lost the following exchange:

> BOY: My name is Pancho Villa.
> GIRL: Any relation to the bandit chief?

At times history was whitewashed in the censorship of the Hollywood films. Paramount's *Wells Fargo* (1938) lost all references to Mexico's defeat in the Mexican-American War.[18] Brazil censored Columbia's *Plane Devils* (1938) because the script claimed that the Wright Brothers were the first aviators, whereas every Brazilian child knew that the real pioneer of air travel was Santos Dumont. As a result of the growing number of these restrictions, Hollywood's image of the Latin softened as the 1930s progressed, but certain stereotyped notions never quite disappeared.

Warner Brothers' *Bordertown* (1935), directed by Archie Mayo, best reveals the ambivalence with which Hollywood viewed its Latin neighbors. *Bordertown* is no exception to the socially conscious films produced by Warners in the 1930s, for, in many ways, it is one of the few sympathetic portraits of the Mexican-American yet produced. Johnny Ramírez (Paul Muni) studies hard at law school and graduates at the top of his class. Yet, in his first courtroom appearance he succumbs to anger and attacks the defendant. He is then ejected bodily from the court and is disbarred. He is thus driven to the outside of the law and becomes the manager of a gambling casino.

In many ways Ramírez is no different from the others in Warner's stable of Depression gangster heroes as seen in *Little Caesar* (1931) or *Public Enemy* (1931).[19] Yet, he has certain frailties which Hollywood generally considered as characteristic of the Mexican. Whereas Rico and Tommy Powers are cool and calculating, Ramírez is subject to uncontrolled fits of anger which bring his downfall. The viewer is thus asked to believe that Ramírez has studied diligently in night school for several years, but can lose his temper in his first courtroom appearance. This unexpected excitability remained a characteristic of the Latin in film. Lupe Velez became the specific exponent of this trend as a concrete demonstration that Latins are unpredictable, passionate, and uncontrollable. Her film titles (*Hot Pepper* [Fox, 1933], *Strictly Dynamite* [RKO, 1934], and *Mexican Spitfire* [RKO, 1940]) reveal this clearly.

A second aspect of *Bordertown* reveals yet another common stereotype of the Latin during the 1930s. Muni is portrayed as a loner after his fall from grace. At last, one evening in his gambling casino, he meets the society woman who brought his downfall in his first courtroom trial. She is strangely attracted to Ramírez. After a few dates, he resolves to marry her. They go for a ride on a deserted country road, and Johnny pops the question. The heiress appears shocked and replies, "We aren't of the same tribe, savage!" Johnny is irate ("I was O.K. to kiss and have fun with, but not O.K. to marry"). The young woman is disgusted by his outburst and runs away from him. In her haste she runs across the road and is hit by a car and killed. Johnny is sobered by the experience and sells his gambling casino. He then uses the money to establish a law school in his hometown. At last he realizes where he belongs—with his own people—the *chicanos.* He will never try to leave again.

Johnny is thus unable to find love. Only an insane Bette Davis loves him, but he has no sympathy for this madwoman. Despite the mystique of the "Latin Lover" lingering from the 1920s, the Latin men of the 1930s seemed to be incapable of an adult relationship with a woman. Similarly, even if a love affair is brewing, the Latin male will consistently be tossed aside if his flame is confronted by a North American. This occurs in *Flying Down to Rio* (1933) when Raul Roulien willingly steps aside and allows his fiance to marry Gene Raymond, an American bandleader. The sexuality once attributed to Novarro or Valentino in the 1920s seems to have passed to the women in the 1930s, as the Latin maidens in *Border Cafe* (1937) or in *Flying Down to Rio* are able to attract men effortlessly from across a crowded room. The Latin men, however, remain alone and unloved. Ironically, when Raoul Walsh remade *Bordertown* as *They Drive By Night,* starring George Raft as a North American, all of Ramírez's limitations disappeared. Although the main character is still loved by an insane woman, he has his own girl friend whom he intends to marry in the near future.

Third, Johnny Ramírez, unable to succeed in the legal profession, turns outside the law and runs a gambling casino. Again, it seems to have been a common assumption that gambling was the Latin's favorite occupation. During the 1930s the Mexican-American actor, Leo Carrillo, appeared in more than thirty films. In almost half he portrayed a man involved in illicit activities, usually gambling, murder, or the rackets. Even if Carrillo had a legitimate source of money, as in *Girl of the Rio* or in *In Caliente* (WB, 1935), he still was portrayed as bearing an uncontrollable urge to engage in illegal acts. Therefore, Muni's successful rise in the gambling business in *Bordertown* should come as no surprise since these activities were the rule rather than the exception.

The final irony of *Bordertown* was the presence of Paul Muni in the lead role. Covered in a dark shade of pancake makeup, Muni is only portraying a Latin. In order to prepare for the role,

Muni haunted Olvera Street in the Spanish section of Los Angeles, but it was not enough. "I have to go swimming in tequila," he said, and traveled to Mexicali with Carroll Graham, author of the original novel of *Bordertown*. He also began taking private Spanish lessons before the shooting began. Yet, it seems incongruous for a North American of European descent to portray the major Latin roles of the 1930s, while the real Latins languished in minor roles. While Ricardo Cortez may have played the romantic lead in several films of the period, his name is misleading. In reality he was Jacob Kranz of Budapest. Thus, false Latins found the road to success easier than real Latins in the 1930s.

The basic assumption of Latin homogeneity allowed this practice to continue, as dark skin and bulging white eyeballs seemed the prime qualification for a Latin role. More often than not, these characteristics could be supplied in the makeup room. The Latin women suffered similarly. Although, unlike their male counterparts, Latin women might achieve leading roles, there was no guarantee that they would portray a citizen of their appropriate country. The slightly darker skin seemed to allow the women to portray *any* minority without the slightest respect for geographical bounds. For example, Lupe Velez commented that she had portrayed "Chinese, Eskimos, Japs, squaws, Hindus, Swedes, Malays, and Javanese."[20] She came somewhat closer to home in *Kongo* (1931), where she portrayed a Portuguese adrift in Africa, but even then her Spanish accent must have tickled Brazilian audiences. It was not until the 1940s that Lupe Velez achieved a firm screen identity as a Mexican in her *Mexican Spitfire* series.

The presence of Latins in disguise became so frequent that even Al Jolson commented about it in song in Warner Brothers' musical *Go into Your Dance* (1935). Jolson sings his praise to Señorita Dolores Menéndez, "the premiere dancer of Spain" in "She's a Latin from Manhattan":*

Fate sent her to me over the sea from Spain
And she's the one in a million for me.
I found my romance when she went dancing by,
And she must be a Castilian, si, si.

Is she from Havana or Madrid?
But something about her is making me doubt her,
I think I remember the kid.

She's a Latin from Manhattan
I can tell by her mañana
She's a Latin from Manhattan,
And not Havana.

Though she does a rumba for us
And calls herself Dolores,
She was in a Broadway chorus
Known as Susie Donahue.

Only one film of the 1930s attempted to avoid the stereotypes that *Bordertown* so clearly exemplified. Ironically, the film that most closely mirrored a Latin reality and treated its characters with dignity was a bubbly musical, *Flying Down to Rio* (1933), produced by RKO, the same studio that released the offensive *Girl of the Rio* a year earlier. Rockefeller interests had recently gained control of the film company. With considerable investments in Venezuela and the rest of South America, the family seemed to have more sensitivity for the Latin character, a sentiment that soon became studio policy. The RKO studio thus became one of the few to ban stereotypes offensive to Latin countries, and Nelson himself ordered the budget for *Flying Down to Rio* tripled.[21]

Flying Down to Rio remains totally different from all other films that concern Latin America in the 1930s. Other films presented backwater border towns, with few buildings, a local militia, and a large but lazy peasantry. Suddenly, this film presents the cosmopolitan city of Rio de Janeiro as it really is. Although not filmed in the city itself, *Flying Down to Rio* possesses several location sequences shot by RKO photographers which capture the scenic beauty of the city and its tropical beaches. Here, the main characters, Dolores Del Rio and Raul Roulien (actually a

Brazilian), differ little from the figures that populated other comedies of the 1930s. They are sophisticated, warm, and polite, and, indeed, no different from their North American counterparts. Additionally, the musical chorus in the film reflected Brazil's multiracial society with great accuracy. The Carioca, the film's classic dance number, is performed by all of the racially mixed groups—whites, blacks, mulattoes, mestizos—which actually comprise Brazilian society.[22]

Despite a generally accurate portrayal of a Latin reality in *Flying Down to Rio,* the film remained the exception rather than the rule. The stereotypic conceptions represented by *Bordertown* governed almost all films concerning or starring Latin characters in the 1930s. Ironically, the protests from the Latin American countries failed to improve the situation during this period. Rather than utilize the option of blocking all of a production company's films if a feature offended national sentiments, censors chose to remove questionable dialogue or scenes. Of twenty films censored in Mexico from 1937 to 1939, only four were banned outright. Of the remaining sixteen, several judicious deletions made them suitable for national viewing.[23] Perhaps the major reason that Latin countries failed to follow through with the strident rhetoric of the reciprocal treaties of 1935 and 1936 was the lack of a substitute local product. Hollywood had abandoned the production of Spanish-speaking films only in 1935, and the local companies had yet to fill the gap caused by their absence by 1938. Thus, despite continued irritation over Hollywood's treatment of the Latin character, South American countries were still unable to enforce their strict censorship goals.

It took a world war to reverse the continued practice of abuses from Hollywood. By 1938 Germany began to produce Spanish-language films for the first time. While the first productions (*The Barber of Seville* [Hispano-Film Corp.] and *Andalusian Nights* [UFA]) remained light operettas, the Reich soon began distributing newsreels and propaganda films in the Spanish markets. A typical short, released in Panama, revealed "large German populations in Chile, Argentina, and Brazil, and how they controlled commerce and industry in certain regions."[24] At the same time in southern South America, domestic Nazi groups managed to prevent the showing of anti-Nazi or pro-American films. *The Confessions of a Nazi Spy* (WB, 1939) was banned by the provincial governor of Santiago, Chile, as "likely to create public disorder," while such films as the British *The Lion Has Wings* (1939) were disrupted by audience riots or the throwing of stink bombs. In this city pro-Nazi films were shown virtually without hindrance, as all Germans and German-Chileans were ordered to attend. If not, the *New York Times* reported, they might be blacklisted or lose their jobs. Still worse were cases of relatives in Germany being harassed if one did not attend such propaganda films as *Baptism by Fire* (1939) which used "the German invasion of Poland in an effort to create an impression of the irresistible power of the German military machine."[25]

While Germany was crowding Hollywood films out of Latin markets on both an ideological and economic plane, the American film industry faced yet another crisis which tightened its dependence on South America. The growing war in Europe sharply decreased the foreign film revenues which were often necessary to ensure a film's profit. Only Latin America remained as a prime market for American film exports.[26] Thus, Hollywood's fate became tied to a region it had formerly scorned or ignored and the years of World War II became the era of Hollywood's "Good Neighbor" Policy. Latin characters, themes, music, and dance suddenly invaded American films in an attempt to conquer the new markets.

THE FILMS AND THE STARS

Dolores Del Rio

> She is naturally friendly and vivacious and she needs people around her in a casual manner. It was heartbreaking for her to discover that most people, following an introduction, backed off and looked at her as though she were the sacred ceiling of Sistine Chapel.
>
> *Photoplay*, December, 1934

Lupe Velez represented the violent, hot-tempered Latin to the extreme. Dolores Del Rio manifested the same passions, the same deep emotions, but she kept them within her. While Lupe erupted, Dolores smoldered and seethed. Lupe went and got her man, while Dolores need only flicker her eyelash or arch her brow in order to attract the man of her dreams. In *Flying Down to Rio,* Gene Raymond, a bandleader, glances across a crowded dance floor. In the back of the room he spots Dolores sitting at a table. She lowers her eyes and peeps at him through the lattice of her fingers. Raymond is hers forever.

Dolores exalted her style of romance: "Life does not hurt the sheltered woman. There are no disillusionments, no rash disappointments for her to suffer through. She knows only the sweet beauty of love and the joy of her own calm domesticity."[27] The actions of Lupe and the sex-mad flappers of the 1920s shocked her: "I am always amazed how quickly an American girl can get over a broken romance. In my country, the Latin girl has been known to pine away, in quiet solitude, until she died. It is really beautiful and very sentimental to suffer for love, no?"

Born of an aristocratic Mexican family in 1905, Dolores was raised in a semicolonial fashion in Durango until the revolutionary leader, Pancho Villa, sacked the town. The family escaped to Mexico City in extreme haste. Dolores's cloistered upbringing resulted in a view of male-female relationships that hearkened to medieval Spain.

She explained: "In my country, love does not come quickly. It is inspired by starlight and flowers and gentle music. When the young man comes to call on a señorita in Mexico, he brings his guitar. He stands in the patio at first, playing tender melodies until he knows that she is willing to respond. He waits for her to come to the grilled window and look down at him. Then he kisses a white rose and throws it to her. After that, he might dare to hope for a further interest, if she kisses the flower and tosses it back to him."

Dolores Del Rio's view would certainly offend the women's

liberationists of today. She believed that men's desire to "protect women is their highest privilege. The American girl has her freedom, true. But I think she cheats herself of the chivalry which men in my country display. And that is too bad, no?"

Ironically, Dolores's confessions to *Photoplay* contrast vividly with her real love life. This is not surprising, since words and actions rarely coincide, especially in Hollywood. The interesting fact is that the picture of colonial romance that Dolores has offered to her fans almost perfectly matches her *film* image in the early 1930s.

Dolores's real life is hardly as pristine as she would like to imagine it. At the age of fifteen she graduated from a convent school and married Jaime Martínez del Río, of a prominent Castilian family. Edwin Carewe, a Hollywood director, met Dolores at a party in Mexico where she danced the tango. He was entranced and invited her to Hollywood for a screen test. As she became successful in such films as Raoul Walsh's *What Price Glory?* (Fox, 1926), *Resurrection* (UA, 1927), and *Ramona* (UA, 1928), her husband succumbed to a typical Hollywood syndrome. As he became known as Mr. Dolores Del Rio, their marriage went on the rocks. A failure as a playwright, Jaime died in a sanatorium under mysterious circumstances. His death was listed as "blood poisoning following a minor operation," but some believed it suicide since it followed so soon after Dolores's attempt to divorce him.

In a surprise move, Dolores broke with Carewe and signed with Joseph Schenck and United Artists. Shortly thereafter she married Cedric Gibbons, an MGM art director. She fell sick after their honeymoon, and her United Artists contract was canceled due to a clause which stated that the star may not be absent from the set for more than a month. Her bright future became cloudy, as many assumed she had suffered a nervous breakdown because of her first husband's death and her rapid remarriage. A fan magazine lamented: "Dolores, mother of pain—oh, she was born under an ill-fated star, a star of suffering."[28]

Dolores explained her fall in more tragic terms:

All of my most frightful troubles came when I was at the height of my
career. Jaime was thrilled at first by my success. We both thought that
he would achieve success too, in pictures. But gradually he came to hate
me because I had succeeded and he had not. It was terrible for both of
us. . . . *Everything* happened to me. Tragic, terrifying things: I lived in a
hotbed of intrigue, politics, of lies and malice, of cross currents of
human purposes. I was hurt so often, I was afraid to express myself.[29]

Matters calmed down after 1933 as she fulfilled contracts first
with RKO and then with Warner Brothers. Her film persona
betrayed none of the turbulence of her daily life. Rather, it in-
voked the Spanish romantic idealism of her childhood.

At first it seemed that Dolores Del Rio might follow in the
footsteps of Lupe Velez, as a dark-skinned stand-in for any
minority figure on the screen. She played a Hawaiian maiden in
Bird of Paradise (RKO, 1932). David O. Selznick reportedly told
King Vidor, the director, "I don't care what story you use as long
as we call it *Bird of Paradise,* and Del Rio jumps into a flaming
volcano at the finish."[30] Fortunately, *Flying Down to Rio* saved
Dolores from this fate.

In this early Fred Astaire and Ginger Rogers musical, Dolores
Del Rio appears as one of the screen's most beautiful women.
She is so attractive to men that one chorus girl asks, "What do
these South American girls have below the Equator that we
haven't?" Dolores never pursues her men, they always come to
her. She attracts them by a very subtle form of flirting. ("Flirting
is a fine art with Mexican girls. They are never alone with men, so
they must find secret little ways of letting a man know they are
interested in him," Dolores explained.)[31]

The character that Dolores establishes in this film shaped her
later screen portrayals. She is always a lady, and more often
than not, an aristocrat. In *In Caliente* (1935), she is one of the
world's greatest dancers; in *I Live for Love* (WB, 1935) she is one
of the greatest actresses.

Among the Latin women on the screen in the 1930s, Dolores
is the lady. Habitually dressed in long, white gowns, the role of

the peasant, so common to other Latin women, seems impossible for her. While she differs from her sister performers in her aristocratic bearing, she retains one factor in common with them. She is irresistibly attracted to North American men. Latin males have no chance with her. At best, as in *Flying Down to Rio,* they are portrayed as good sports, who allow their fiancee to marry the man she really loves.

While this occurs in almost all of Del Rio's films of this period, Busby Berkeley's *I Live for Love* illustrates it best. At first Donna Alvarez (Dolores Del Rio) loves Rico (Don Alvarado), a Latin, so much so that she insists he perform opposite her in her next play. The producers despise Rico, a pathetic actor, and instead, cast Roger Kerry (Everett Marshall), who has walked into the theater by accident, as Donna's co-star.

Donna refuses to perform with Kerry and Rico is eventually given the part. During the film, Donna continually fights with Kerry, who has become a popular radio singer. Finally, Roger sings to Donna and she melts in his arms. Rico is forgotten immediately. They decide to marry, but Donna refuses to give up her stage career. They argue again, and Donna resolves to marry Rico for spite. Roger meets Donna at the door of the church and they run away from the wedding leaving Rico in the lurch. Thus, although Del Rio is a full woman, the Latin male, whether Rico, Johnny Ramírez (*Bordertown*), or Julio Rubeiro (*Flying Down to Rio*), has yet to come into his own.

Wallace Beery in *Viva Villa!*

The complexity of the Mexican Revolution and the heroic image of Pancho Villa seem to have sent screenwriter Ben Hecht and director Jack Conway into a state of dithering confusion. The period of 1910 to 1917 appears so chaotic to the creators of *Viva Villa!* (MGM, 1934) that conventional narrative style is virtually abandoned in sheer hopelessness. Thus, in order to convey the intricate shifts in political moods, sectional alliances, and class divisions, Hecht resorts to the most extensive use of title cards since the silent era. As the film progresses, the process of political change is presented wholly by the title cards. The audience feels that it is reading *Viva Villa!* rather than seeing a film account of the Mexican Revolution.

While this "visual novel" presents the politics of the period, the film itself concerns the private life of the revolutionary hero, Pancho Villa (Wallace Beery). Hecht's screenplay, however, presents Villa as an unlikely hero. The film's Villa is an illiterate, murderous, unscrupulous woman chaser, whose only virtue is a blind loyalty to Francisco Madero. But then, as the first of many title cards warns:

> The saga of the Mexican hero does not come out
> of historical truth, but of legend.

Thus, from the first moment of the film, Hecht abandons all attempts to convey an historical reality. Instead, Villa becomes a fantastic creature, who resembles Hollywood's stock portrayal of the violent Latin rather than a representation of the actual historical figure.

The film begins in a regional courthouse during the Porfiriato. The magistrate is bored, for once again the peasants have stolen food from the estate of Don Miguel. Although the crime is officially a misdemeanor, the peasants are executed by hanging in the central plaza. Villa's troops arrive and bring the bodies of the dead peasants into the courtroom and prop them up in the jury box. Villa declares that there will be a second trial, with the corpses as the jury. Naturally, the magistrates are sentenced to death, and Villa and his top aide (Leo Carrillo) murder the justices and the previous jury. Carrillo, however, is upset by Villa's mock trial: "I don't like it[justice] — it takes too long."

> Out of the orgy of cruelty and avarice which
> made Mexico a land of half slaves arose a hero,
> the Christ-fool, Francisco Madero.

Madero summons Pancho Villa to an informal meeting:

Villa: I'm Pancho Villa, the bandit. You sent for me?

MADERO: No, I sent for Pancho Villa, the peón, whose father was whipped to death, whose sister was ravished, and the man who the peones worship.

Madero brings Pancho into his confidence. He shows the rebel a map of Mexico ("Eet looks like a sombrero turned upside-down"), and explains his plans for the country's future: "I want an army of liberty to bring peace and justice to Mexico." Villa embraces Madero, and exclaims, "You bring great dreams to my heart."

> Chaos hit Mexico and at the head of the chaos
> rode Pancho Villa with a cry of vengeance.

Scenes of death and devastation are seen behind the title card. Once again Madero summons Villa. He is displeased because Villa's troops have killed wounded men on the battlefield. Madero calls him a bandit, and claims that he has brought disgrace on the Revolution. Villa leaves in disgust, shouting, "You need hate to win a Revolution." As he stalks from the room, Madero laments: "He's a child! A bad child! Yet he knows how much I need him." Villa sheepishly returns, wearing Beery's inimitable grin, and agrees to submit his troops to the control of General Pascal.

Pascal becomes envious of the military successes of the peasant general, and schemes to have Villa arrested for theft and executed. Madero hears of this plot and pardons Villa. Pascal announces the pardon at the last possible moment, after "ready" and "aim," but before "fire." Villa is freed, but the price is exile from his native Mexico.

> Villa's soul grows small in a gringo saloon.

Pascal's power grows, and he shoots Madero as he is writing to his "only friend," Pancho Villa. Villa hears the news of his mentor's assassination, and he immediately decides to sober up and come to the aid of the ailing revolution. His troops regather as soon as Villa returns to Mexico. Their new battle cry becomes "Viva Villa!"

> *Somebody had stolen their revolution and hate*
> *thundered out of the cactus fields. An army of*
> *vengeance arose out of nowhere to recapture the*
> *land stolen from their fathers.*

With Madero gone, Villa reverts to his former habits:

> *Villa fought in his own way—the vanquished*
> *were slaughtered—the wounded slain.*

Carrillo returns to his general's side. In an economy move, he lines up his victims in groups of three before he shoots them. In this manner, the bloodthirsty lieutenant manages to save two bullets. Villa captures Pascal's fortress. The disgraced general begs Villa to shoot him immediately. Villa, however, recalls how Pascal saved the letter of pardon at his execution until the last moment. Eager for revenge, he pours bottles of honey over Pascal and buries him in an anthill. As Pascal screams in agony, Villa sits down to a breakfast of coffee and toast. Fortunately, Pascal's lengthy demise remains offscreen.

> *Pancho Villa enters Mexico City as a conqueror*
> *at the head of an army of 60,000.*

Stock footage of Villa's actual entrance into Mexico City is shown with Wallace Beery's image superimposed. Villa assumes the presidency, but discovers that he is incapable of performing such a lofty job. He commits blunders from his first moment in office. He hires a private firm to print one billion dollars in new Mexican notes with his picture on the bills, but he cannot understand why the printers will not accept this currency as payment. Villa finally realizes that he would prefer "riding a horse in Chihuahua" to being president of Mexico. He returns to his hometown, and shortly thereafter he is assassinated on the way to the butcher shop to buy pork chops for dinner. Villa's dying words explain his violent ways: "Goodbye my Mexico. Forgive me for my crimes. If I sinned against you, it is because I loved you too much."

> *He had not fought in vain. A new Mexico based*
> *on justice and equality had arisen.*

Unfortunately, this new Mexican land is never seen. The audience leaves the theater with an image of Mexico as a violent land, and Pancho Villa as an unlikely hero. Hecht's Villa retains the traits that Latin countries had always abhorred. His penchant for violence, his lust for women, and his tendency toward drink overshadow by far his one virtue that emerges on the screen—his loyalty. Although Wallace Beery's portrayal makes Villa almost an agreeable character, there is no advance in the image of the Mexican from that of the silent era.

RKO's *Hi Gaucho*

RKO hit the heights and the depths in the depiction of the Latin in the films of the 1930s. *Flying Down to Rio* displayed exquisite care in its overview of Brazilian society. *Girl of the Rio,* on the other hand, offended virtually every country of Latin America with the portrayal of the drunken, vile, and power hungry Señor Tostado.

More often than not, the RKO films achieved a middle ground with a mixture of good intentions and hopeless stereotypes. *Hi Gaucho* (1936) best represents the Hollywood confusion when faced with Latin American characters. Typically, the starring roles were filled by non-Latins, John Carroll (Lucio), Rod La Rocque (Escurra), and Steffi Duna (Inez).

The film is set in the "Early Argentine—The Land of the Gauchos," which strangely resembles the wild west of other RKO features. A band of gauchos ride by, dressed in authentic native costume. They are prone to song and sing of their love of freedom—let's enjoy the happy days now and not worry about tomorrow; let's worry about tomorrow tomorrow. Their "Song of the Open Road" is hardly Latin in style. It bears more resemblance to Rudolph Friml's Mountie melodies from *Rose Marie.*

The gauchos find a coach on the road driven by an Argentine so illiterate that he is unable to construct plurals in his own language. More than likely, it is the fault of the screenwriters, rather than the character himself. Lucio, the leader, discovers a beautiful maiden in the coach. At first Doña Inez calls him a barbarian, but he kisses her and she immediately falls in love with him ("I liked eet").

Lucio returns to his father, Don Valero, and tells him that he is "crazy with love." He is determined to marry the young woman.

Complications arise. Inez is the daughter of Doña Vicenta, arch rival of Don Valero. She would never allow her daughter to marry a "barbaric gaucho." Furthermore, Inez has been unknowingly betrothed to Don Salvador De Aragón, as part of a financial arrangement with Doña Vicenta.

The bandit Escurra and his gaucho henchmen arrive on the scene. They kidnap the elderly Salvador and Escurra takes his place. This is an easy task since neither Inez nor her mother has seen the intended groom. Escurra hopes to marry into this rich Argentine family and steal the Vicenta fortune.

Inez, however, refuses to marry him: "I am young. I want love, romance, the right to choose." Doña Vicenta chides her daughter for bearing such silly notions. Inez sneaks from the house and meets Lucio in a cantina. After a brief tango, Inez and Lucio decide to marry.

Escurra's disguise is revealed before the wedding ceremony. Doña Vicenta and Valero resolve their differences and the children are free to marry.

This simple plot perpetuates several common stereotypes of Latins in films of this period. The young Latin men and women seemingly ooze sensuality. Attraction between men and women is immediate and irresistible. A mere kiss becomes a bond for life. While sensuality is exalted, the Latin American law enforcement machinery is ridiculed continually. A short, fat general controls the troops who are easily outwitted by Lucio. The general talks unwittingly to the bandit Escurra who is disguised as Salvador. The general explains that he will catch the bandit easily, because he can tell an evil man by the shape of his ears! He notices nothing unusual about the bogus Salvador and stupidly walks away from the real villain.

Yet, despite these flaws, the author-director (Tommy Atkins) makes extraordinary attempts to explain Argentine culture to the audience. There is a lengthy discussion of the *mate* (tea) drinking ritual. The extras speak in Spanish rather than in the usual broken English. Finally, there is little of the violence so common among Latins in films of the silent era. All disputes are settled amicably and reasonably. *Hi Gaucho* thus has a well-meaning tone which is indicative of the coming trend of sympathetic portrayals of Latin Americans in the 1940s, the era of Hollywood's Good Neighbor Policy. Indeed, by 1939, Warner Brothers presents a film version of the life of the Mexican President Benito Juárez, and suddenly all the bandits seem to disappear.

NOTES

1. See: George Roeder, "The Image of the Mexican," unpublished manuscript, University of Wisconsin, 1971.

2. *New York Times* (*NYT*), August 18, 1929, II, 21.

3. *La Prensa* (Buenos Aires, Argentina), April 27, 1930.

4. *NYT,* November 18, 1929, p. 7.

5. Ibid., August 7, 1938, IX, 4.

6. For an account of the American venture into the Spanish-language market see Emilio García Riera, *Historia documental del cine mexicano* (Mexico City, 1969), I, 9–17.

7. *NYT,* May 25, 1930, IX, 4.

8. See Domingo di Núbila, *Historia del cine argentino* (Buenos Aires, 1959), I, 39–99, and Adhemar Gonzaga, *70 Años de Cinema Brasileiro* (Rio de Janeiro, 1966), pp. 53–85.

9. *NYT,* May 17, 1932, II, 17.

10. Ibid., December 19, 1932, p. 16.

11. See DeWitt Bodeen, "Dolores Del Rio," *Films in Review* (May, 1967), pp. 266–283.

12. See Frank J. Taylor, "Leo the Caballero," *Saturday Evening Post,* July 6, 1946, p. 26.

13. *NYT,* May 9, 1932.

14. Ibid., April 20, 1932, p. 27.

15. See League of Nations, *Treaty Series,* vol. 165 (1935), no. 3818.

16. See John Eugene Harley, *World-Wide Influences of the Cinema: A Study of Official Censorship and the International Cultural Aspects of Motion Pictures* (Los Angeles, 1940), Chap. V.

17. *NYT,* April 1, 1934, p. 29; April 15, X, 4; and September 7, p. 25.

18. Frederick C. Turner, *The Dynamic of Mexican Nationalism* (Chapel Hill, 1968), p. 299.

19. See Andrew Bergman, *We're in the Money* (New York, 1971).

20. *Saturday Evening Post,* January 2, 1932, p. 26.

21. Russ Merritt, *Marquee Theatre* (Madison, Wisc., 1971), p. 17.

22. Arlene Croce, *The Fred Astaire and Ginger Rogers Book* (London, 1972), p. 25.

23. Hurley, *World-Wide Influences,* pp. 163–167.

24. *NYT,* February 13, 1938, p. 16, and November 12, p. 6.

25. Ibid., July 16, 1940.

26. *Variety,* September 3, 1940, p. 6.

27. *Photoplay,* April, 1934, p. 39, for this quotation and those in the following paragraphs.

28. Ibid., August, 1931, p. 102.

29. Bodeen, *"Dolores Del Rio,"* p. 271.

30. Tony Thomas and Tim Terry, *The Busby Berkeley Book* (New York, 1973), p. 45.

31. *Photoplay,* April, 1934, p. 39.

Courtesy of the Wisconsin Center for Film and Theater Research.

Paul Muni in "Bordertown"

Courtesy of the Wisconsin Center for Film and Theater Research.

Paul Muni in the title role in "Juarez"

Courtesy of the Wisconsin Center for Film and Theater Research.

Dolores Del Rio and Ricardo Cortez in "Wonder Bar"

Courtesy of the Wisconsin Center for Film and Theater Research.

Dolores Del Rio in "In Caliente"

Carmen Miranda in "The Gang's All Here"

The Miranda Impersonators: Betty Grable in "Down Argentine Way"

The Miranda Impersonators: "Winged Victory" (1944)

Marlon Brando and Jean Peters in "Viva Zapata!"

4

HOLLYWOOD'S
GOOD NEIGHBOR POLICY

THE MOVIES GO TO WAR
1939–1945

My friends, I extend felicitations,
To our South American relations.
May we never leave behind us
All the common ties that bind us.
One hundred and thirty million people
Send regards to you . . .

"Chica Chica Boom Chic" sung by
Don Ameche in *That Night in Rio**

Suddenly in 1939 films utilizing Latin stars, Locales, and historical heroes flooded American screens. Such eminent leaders
as Benito Juárez and Simón Bolívar were immortalized on film.
Talent scouts brought planeloads of Latin American talent to
Hollywood, as viewers discovered and delighted in Carmen
Miranda, Desi Arnaz, and Cesar Romero. Films also began to
differentiate between varying South American locales, allowing

*Copyright © 1941, renewed 1968, 20th Century Music Corp. Rights throughout
the world controlled by Miller Music Corp. Used by permission.

viewers to spend a *Weekend in Havana* (20th, 1941), or *Midnight in Mexico* (RKO, 1948), or travel *Down Argentine Way* (20th, 1940).

The reason for this deluge of films with Latin American themes may be partly attributed to deliberate government policy. With the growing threat of war with Germany, the United States appeared eager to ease any remaining tensions with South American governments in order to maintain hemispheric unity as a bulwark against foreign invasion. Roosevelt thus attempted to resurrect the "Good Neighbor Policy" which had been ignored in the 1930s in the face of the Mexican government's expropriation of American oil companies and American intervention for political reasons in Nicaragua and Cuba. Anxious to smooth these differences, Roosevelt explained the basis for his vigorous reassertion of the Good Neighbor Policy: "I began to visualize a wholly new attitude toward other American Republics based on an honest and sincere desire, first, to remove from their minds all fear of American aggression—territorial or financial—and, second, to take them into a kind of hemispheric partnership in which no Republic would take undue advantage."[1]

While all government agencies were expected to support the official policy of inter-American unity, a major effort was expected from the Office of the Coordinator of Inter-American Affairs and its director Nelson Rockefeller.[2] Rockefeller appointed a former associate and current vice-president of the Museum of Modern Art to head the Motion Picture Section of this office. John Hay ("Jock") Whitney seemed an appropriate candidate for the position since he recognized the unique role of film in the promotion of inter-American understanding. He explained:

The Office of the Coordinator of Inter-American Affairs has a share in the task of imparting the full force of the meaning of freedom and sovereignty to a quarter of a billion people in the Americas. The menace of Nazism and its allied doctrines, its techniques and tactics, must be understood from Hudson Bay to Punta Arenas. Wherever the motion picture can do a basic job of spreading the gospel of the Americas' common stake in this struggle, there that job must and shall be done.[2]

Similarly, the Hays Office, which controlled film censorship, also appointed an expert in Latin American affairs in order to avoid blatant errors which might offend the "neighbors to the South." Will Hays declared that the appointment of Addison Durland to this post would "be another step in the motion picture industry's cooperation in current events to promote hemispheric solidarity."[4] This was not mere hyperbole, since Durland, director of NBC's Spanish division, spoke the language fluently and held a degree from the Universidad Nacional de Cuba.

Although the activities of the Motion Picture Section were primarily regulatory, the office also participated in the production of several newsreels and short subjects.[5] Rockefeller and Whitney were instrumental in the hiring of Walt Disney "as the first Hollywood producer of motion pictures specifically intended to carry a message of democracy and friendship below the Rio Grande." Whitney claimed that Disney would show "the truth about the American way," and another executive proclaimed him "the greatest goodwill ambassador of all time." He added that "people all over the world know Disney and love his characters." Therefore, "they would believe Disney's message of Americanism."[6]

Although the Motion Picture Section proclaimed that this was "in no wise a propaganda project," memos from the executive division, published after the war, reveal otherwise. The program directors suggested a series of "direct propaganda films" couched in the simplicity of the animation medium ("If anyone wants details, let him buy a book!"). The films were to stress the following ideals:

1. "WE HAVE MORE FOOD" (Supremacy of the United States in Agriculture. Show on a grand scale the immense agricultural resources of our hemisphere.)

2. "WE HAVE MORE MEN" (Supremacy of the United States in Man Power. . . . While essentially a simplified visual lesson in demography, underlying this film would be a warm feeling of inter-racial friendship and solidarity, aimed at counteracting the Axis propaganda about Uncle Sam's racial prejudices.)

3. "WE ARE IN THE RIGHT."

4. "ALL FOR ONE AND ONE FOR ALL" (We would hand at least one bouquet to every Latin Country by telling and showing them what each country is contributing towards Victory.)

5. "HEMISPHERIC DEFENSE" (A film like this, making strategic considerations vividly clear, could be used to soften up recalcitrant minorities opposed to necessary U.S. bases.)

6. "HITLER THE ANTI-CHRIST" (We close on the Cross triumphant over the Swastika).[7]

The most urgent priority of the Rockefeller Committee was the creation of new symbols expressing the importance of the relationship between the Latin nations and the United States: "Right now we need to create "Pan-Americana," a noble female figure, bearing a torch and a cross, subtly suggesting both the Virgin Mary and the Goddess of Liberty."[8] While the Committee desired Miss Pan-Americana, they received Joe Carioca, a pugnacious Brazilian parrot, who appeared in the Disney animated films *Saludos Amigos* (1943) and *The Three Caballeros* (1945).

The Rockefeller Committee also sponsored the showings of Hollywood films with vigorous statements of the democratic way "in American embassies and Ministries throughout South America." The South American "diplomatic circuit" thus saw such films as *Confessions of a Nazi Spy, Young Mr. Lincoln* (20th, 1939), *Abe Lincoln in Illinois* (RKO, 1940), *Manhunt* (20th, 1941), and *Sergeant York* (WB, 1942). It was estimated that more than thirteen thousand viewed the first six pictures shipped south of the border.[9]

In addition to these direct propaganda functions, both the Office of the Coordinator of Inter-American Affairs and the Hays Office provided technical assistance whenever necessary, and applied pressure if studios depicted Latins in an unfavorable light. For example, Whitney convinced Twentieth Century–Fox to spend $40,000 in order to reshoot scenes from *Down Argentine Way* (1940) which erroneously described native customs.[10] Whitney's office also encouraged Hollywood stars to travel to Latin America in order to spread goodwill and reassert the government's commitment to hemispheric unity. In the first flush of enthusiasm Alice Faye, Wallace Beery, and Ann Sheridan announced their intention to visit South America, but Whitney scrapped these plans after a Douglas Fairbanks junket proved a disaster, as the star inadvertently offended everyone he met.[11]

Thus, the onus of the production of films promoting American unity lay on Hollywood's doorstep. The response of the studio executives was indeed surprising, as the seven major studios were in the midst of an expensive antitrust suit brought by the government, which sought to prevent the monopolistic practices of "block booking" and "blind selling" which forced theater owners to purchase films in groups from the distributors without any knowledge of the relative merits of the films nor the ability to reject any in the package.[12] Despite the resentment over the government's suit, Hollywood fervently responded to the patriotic call and produced Latin-themed motion pictures in unprecedented numbers.[13]

Yet, Hollywood's rationale for the resurrection of films with Latin themes betrayed a complex of motives. Patriotism, an emotion that has been muted in this day and age, seemed quite alive in the prewar era. Films not only promoted the importance of national unity in the face of a foreign threat, but also actively encouraged the entry of the United States into this hitherto European war. Despite protestations to the contrary, filmmakers made no pretense of neutrality in the period before Pearl Harbor.

The isolationist forces in the Senate, led by Gerald Nye, brought Hollywood to task for its production of so-called "propaganda" films which encouraged American entry into the war. The inquiry of the Subcommittee of the Interstate Commerce Commission was fortunately brief, aborted by the attack on Pearl Harbor which naturally stilled debates on isolationism. Nevertheless, studio executives faced this hostile inquisition with profound courage. For example, one of the first witnesses was Harry M. Warner, president of Warner Brothers, which produced *Sergeant York, Confessions of a Nazi Spy, Juarez* (WB, 1939), and other films which glorified United States participation in wars which defended democracy and freedom. Warner, confident of his principles, made no attempt to disguise his personal feelings. He testified:

I am opposed to nazi-ism. I abhor and detest every principle and practice of the Nazi movement. To me, nazi-ism typifies the very opposite of the kind of life every decent man, woman, and child wants to live. I believe nazi-ism is a world revolution whose ultimate objective is to destroy our democracy, wipe out all religion, and enslave our people. . . . I am ready to give myself and all personal resources to aid in the defeat of the Nazi menace to the American people.[14]

The testimony of Warner, Darryl F. Zanuck, and other studio executives ostensibly reveals a patriotic motive for the production of films designed to encourage American participation in the war. Consequently, it might be argued that studios manifested a similar disposition to produce films about Latin America in order to promote hemispheric unity.

Nevertheless, certain economic motives might have also encouraged the studios' receptivity to films concerning Latin America. To a certain extent, this wave of Latin films was a response to the new interest in South American music and dances. Arthur Freed, mentor of the MGM musicals, expressed the desire to produce In Gay Havana (uncompleted) and explained:

I believe that hemispheric solidarity, good neighborliness, and the like is only a background reason for the flood of South American features. . . . The actual reason is South American music. . . . Swing music which has held the center stage for five to six years is now passing out and the rhumba stuff is jumping into the number one position in American taste.[15]

Despite Hollywood's willingness to follow such popular trends, a more basic economic rationale can be discerned for the production of films with Latin themes. The coming of the war in Europe drastically lessened the influx of foreign film revenues. Certain countries, conquered by the Germans, banned American films outright. Others, such as Britain and Australia, needed foreign exchange so desperately that they decreed a 50 percent reduction in the amount spent for American films.[16] A sketch of the major foreign film markets reveals the precarious situation, since, by 1940, only Britain remained as an importer of American

MAJOR FOREIGN MARKETS (1939)

Country	Percentage of total foreign revenue
Great Britain	45.0
France/Belgium	13.0
Austria	11.2
Poland	1.0
Bulgaria/Greece/Turkey	1.2

MARKETS MOST LIKELY TO IMPROVE

Japan	1.3
Scandinavia	4.2
Central and South America	9.0
Holland	1.5

SOURCE: *Variety*, September 3, 1940, p. 6

films (see chart). In 1939 hopes for future markets centered on four areas: Japan, Holland, Scandinavia, and Central and South America. Again, by 1940, only Central and South America remained as major importers of American films owing to the changing political situation. In order to compensate for lost foreign revenues, Hollywood began to look toward Latin America for economic relief, and actively seek this budding market's share of the film dollar. Thus, the film capital's Good Neighbor Policy reflected more than a patriotic gesture in response to government pressure.

Hollywood's New Sensitivity

Good night, Good Neighbor
This evening with you has charmed me so.
Tomorrow those Latin eyes aglow,
Will haunt me all day.

We're back at your door,
And now we kiss.
Though down in Brazil you'd frown at this
You'll soon learn our ways.

Sung by Dennis Morgan in
Thank Your Lucky Stars (WB, 1943)*

Hollywood's attitude toward the Latin countries suddenly bordered on reverence. *Juarez,* the first film of the South American cycle, offered a panegyric to a nineteenth-century Mexican president, and portrayed him as an equal to Abraham Lincoln.

Indeed, the shadow of Lincoln haunted this enterprise. Juárez, portrayed by Paul Muni, rarely appeared in his office without a portrait of the Great Emancipator peering over his shoulder. Similarly, forced to flee before advancing French troops, Juárez removed his portrait of Lincoln from his office before gathering any of his official documents, thus revealing the importance of the American president to him.

This dramatic link between Juárez and Lincoln leads to the suspicion that Juárez is more a symbol than a man. The film's rhetoric enforces this interpretation, as the Mexican president's dialogue transcends the historical and borders on the universal. Juárez becomes the "defender of democratic principles," and Maximilian and Napoleon III represent "the dictators who seize power illegally." Juárez's critique of European imperialism suggests an analogy with the United States in the years before World War II. Indeed, the Mexican president's climactic speech could just as easily have been delivered in Washington, D.C., in 1939 as in Mexico City in 1864: "By what right, señores, do the Great Powers of Europe invade the lands of simple people . . . kill all who do not make them welcome . . . destroy their fields . . . and take the fruit of their toil from those who survive? . . . The world must know the fate of any usurper who sets his foot upon this soil."[17] As a matter of fact, the "political parallels were so closely drawn" that the critic for the *New York Times* commented that it was not at all difficult to "read between the lines."[18]

Although *Juarez* masked an attempt to urge United States participation in the European war, the film avoided blatant stereotypes of the Mexican and revealed a newfound sensitivity toward Latin characters. Juárez was the first "Mexican" hero of the American screen, and Warners assured that he would be portrayed as accurately as possible. Aeneas MacKenzie, one of the film's three screenwriters, left for Mexico City ten months before the initial preparation of the script, although it would have been easy to prepare a scenario from Bertita Harding's *The Phantom Crown* (1934) which Warners had just purchased. During his lengthy visit, MacKenzie read more than seven hundred secondary sources, the President's private and official correspondence, and contemporary newspapers. As a matter of fact, a portion of the film's dialogue was derived from Congressional debates of the period.[19]

Paul Muni prepared for the role with a marked intensity. He even met and interviewed two elderly survivors of the Juarista army, Colonel Gabriel Morena and General Ignacio Velásquez. Muni asked them about Juárez, whether he laughed or cried, what his voice was like, and how they felt when he walked into the room. Reportedly, these interviews played a major role in shaping Muni's performance.[20]

Juarez impressed its intended audience both in the United States and Mexico. President Lázaro Cárdenas urged that the film be presented in the Palace of Fine Arts, the first motion picture so honored. The premiere audience responded warmly to the film's message, and stopped the show with applause when Muni explained the difference between constitutional democracy and despotism.[21] Indeed, the democratic sentiments of *Juarez* were so forcefully expressed that the film became a success in unexpected locales. *Variety* noted that the film did "big biz in India due mainly to its democracy theme and its stress on rule by the people."[22]

It was deemed prudent to cut only one line for the Mexican premiere. In the original version, Juárez leans over the body of the recently executed Maximilian and whispers, "Forgive me." In Mexico, Juárez bent over, moved his lips, and not a sound was heard. This reportedly headed off a confrontation with leftist elements in the audience upset by the prospect of a Mexican president apologizing to an "imperialist aggressor."

With this newfound reverence toward the Latin, Hollywood abruptly reversed old stereotypes. No longer was the Latin considered as an ignorant peasant. In RKO's *They Met in Argentina* (1941) co-star Buddy Ebsen is surprised as everyone from secretaries to ranch hands are able to speak English with only the slightest trace of an accent. Similarly, films began to portray each nation differently, each possessing an individual culture and history. Again Buddy Ebsen is surprised to learn that Argentine immigration patterns in the nineteenth century paralleled those of the United States. In this manner a lengthy historical discourse becomes de rigueur in order to explain the complicated derivation of the name of the *hacendado* Don Enrique de los Santos O'Shea.

Uniting these new images of the Latin was the common assumption that North America and South America were quite similar. For example, the gauchos of *They Met in Argentina* sing the same song that the North American hero sang as a youth on his Texas ranch. The similarity between the two cultures was stressed in order to accentuate the importance of Pan-American unity. The message was often painfully obvious. A critic for *Time* magazine reviewed the finale from Twentieth Century–Fox's *Springtime in the Rockies* (1940) and caustically commented: "The 'Pan-American Jubilee' number attempts to be just that by whipping together: 1. Latin America (Cesar Romero, Carmen Miranda and her band), 2. the United States (Betty Grable, John Payne, Harry James and his band), and 3. Canada (large Technicolor chunks of Lake Louise where the action takes place). Only the addition of an Eskimo and a penguin could have made the show still more hemispheric in scope."[23]

Despite Hollywood's apparent good intentions, filmmakers actually succeeded in replacing one film stereotype with another. Owing to the popularity of the new Latin rhythms — the conga, the samba, the rumba — Latins became identified with their music, and would rarely appear in American musicals without singing the melodies of their native country. These hip-swaying dances, so different from the sedate North American rhythms, gave Latin artists an increased sensuality which Carmen Miranda, Desi Arnaz, and others emphasized in their screen performances. The use of symbolism often accentuated this image. For example, Desi Arnaz appeared bracketed in flames as he sang the main production number in *Too Many Girls* (RKO, 1940), as several college coeds danced at his feet. Busby Berkeley went even further in *The Gang's All Here* (20th, 1943) by surrounding Carmen Miranda with hundreds of dancing girls with six-foot bananas on their heads. These peripatetic phallic symbols led President Getulio Vargas to censor this film in Miranda's native Brazil.[24]

Yet, this new sensuality, an erotic compensation for years of Latin docility on the screen, rarely achieved its desired fulfillment. Despite the aura of the Latin Lover, the performers from South America rarely managed to marry the hero or heroine. In the 1933 film *Flying Down to Rio* the North American bandleader easily steals Dolores Del Rio from the arms of her Brazilian fiance, Raul Roulien. Nothing has changed by 1941, as James Ellison easily woos Maureen O'Hara, playing an Argentine, away from her boyfriend Alberto Vila in *They Met in Argentina*. The same pattern can be seen in *Too Many Girls* and *Pan-Americana* (1945), both from RKO studios. Thus, the North American still maintained a sexual superiority over the South American despite a startling reversal in the Latin image in film.

The Latins Respond

The popularity of these films with Latin locales, plots, and music pleasantly surprised studio executives. *Down Argentine*

Way, the first film of the Latin musical cycle, did "sensational business in New York, and gave the State theater one of its biggest Saturday grosses ever." The *Variety* critic expressed his enthusiasm, noting that "the picture's reception in Latin America would provide studios with an angle on the potentialities of upping income on big pictures with backgrounds of those countries instead of European settings." He then confidently prophesied that this picture would "inspire a new cycle of films in the Amazon, pampas, and Andes regions."[25]

This analysis revealed a common assumption, namely, that the Latin orientation of the plot, locale, or music would be sure to please Latin audiences. In this manner Hollywood continually underestimated Latin audiences by assuming that they could only understand what was familiar to them. For example, when Bud Abbott and Lou Costello appeared in *In the Navy* (Univ, 1941), officials of the Whitney office and Hollywood screenwriters recommended that special title cards be added in order to explain the jokes to South American audiences. A Universal Films executive explained that "Latins have a different sense of humor than film audiences in the United States!" He added: "They take their pictures seriously. If they see a little fat guy poke the Admiral in the rear with a sixteen inch gun, they will get the idea that the Navy is made up of virtually nothing but little fat guys tickling their officers with heavy artillery."[26] In like manner producers reasoned that Latin-oriented films would be easily understandable to South American audiences and consequently of great popularity.

Hollywood's pretensions of inter-American goodwill hardly prepared studio officials for the acerbic response of Latin American critics and audiences since the warm reception for *Juarez* had lulled them into a sense of security. Local representatives of the film companies noted that goodwill gestures might be turning sour when *Argentine Nights* (Univ, 1940) with the Ritz Brothers and the Andrews Sisters was "hooted off the screen" and almost caused a riot in an Argentine theater.[27] *Down Argentine Way* brought similar complaints: Why was

Carmen Miranda portraying an Argentine when she was obviously a Brazilian? Why were Argentines depicted as the owners of a crooked race track and the Americans once again as the good guys?[28]

Latin Americans possessed a double resentment against these films. First, they were annoyed by the misinterpretations of their culture which occurred frequently despite the plethora of technical advisers available to screenwriters. Brazilians were among the most sensitive, resenting any intimation that their nation possessed a substantial Indian population.[29] Even if films ignored this aspect of Latin society, they still had a tendency to show "South American characters in tight-laced pants and long sideburns or shawls and mantillas." "That's museum stuff," sneered one film director.[30]

Second, Latin American critics resented the inter-American unity message which was clearly evident in each film. *Sintonia*, an Argentine weekly, argued that the "United States Goodwill Drive, via films, radio, and the press has taken on the characteristics of a spiritual blitzkrieg prepared in the arsenals of Yankee advertising." Additionally, local filmmakers argued that "this Good Neighbor Policy might become dangerous to us although the United States wishes us no harm." They reasoned that the "Yanqui cine" was "striking a blow" at the nascent Argentine film industry by crowding local productions out of the marketplace since local audiences preferred the more professionally made American films.[31]

Despite Latin criticism from the very beginning of the South American musical cycle, Hollywood continued with these domestically popular films. Although Whitney scrapped his proposed series of Latin American junkets after Douglas Fairbanks's disastrous visit, he still expressed the conviction of "pushing ahead with the plan for hypoing American solidarity via films, despite the conviction in some South American quarters that the whole idea should be dropped."[32] The Hollywood bandwagon continued, and Joe Carioca, Walt Disney's birdlike version of Carmen Miranda, continued his merry dance.

The End of Hollywood's Good Neighbor Policy

> I've seen too many movies,
> And all they prove is
> Too idiotic
> They all insist that South America's exotic,
> When it couldn't be more boring if it tried.
>
> She said with most refreshing candor
> That Carmen Miranda was subversive propaganda,
> And she should rapidly be shot.
> She didn't care a jot,
> Whether people quoted her or not.
>
> "Nina" from Noël Coward's *Sigh No More* (1945)*

The end of the war did more to dampen Hollywood's enthusiasm with Latin-themed films than did complaints from
South America. After the liberation previously closed markets
once again received American films. Business abroad in the
three months following the end of the war exceeded grosses
of the entire year preceding Pearl Harbor. Audiences in France,
Belgium, and the Philippines flocked to theaters in unprecedented numbers in order to escape a war-weary world.[33] This
ended Hollywood's brief dependence on Latin markets.

Adding to the decline in films with Latin themes after the
war was the increased influence of dubbing. Metro-Goldwyn-
Mayer began with *Gaslight* in 1944 and dubbed all future films
with Spanish-speaking New York actors. Paramount swiftly
followed suit with *The Song of Bernadette* (20th, 1944), and the
results were surprising. Second-rate dubbed films managed to
outgross titled classics. Sam Berger, Loewe's regional director
for Latin America, noted that dubbing had led to a 50 to 90
percent increase in business, as dubbed versions of *Gaslight*
and *Bathing Beauty* (MGM, 1944) outgrossed a subtitled *Gone
with the Wind* (MGM, 1939).[34] Chile remained the only exception to this trend, since Chileans, with their strong regional

Spanish accent, found it difficult to understand films dubbed by American Spanish-speaking actors.[35]

The public was also tiring of the barrage of Latin American films. It is not surprising that postwar musical comedies presented songs dealing with the public weariness with South American music. For example, in *Call Me Mister* (1946) Betty Garrett sang "South America, Take It Away," urging the Latins to "take back the rhumba, mambo, and samba" because "her back was aching from all that shaking."

Despite Hollywood's sudden lack of interest in Latin America after the war's end, the filmic Good Neighbor Policy had beneficial and unexpected results. It reversed a thirty-year-old Latin stereotype of the violent, dirty, and lazy South American, and presented a continent with educated classes and indigenous tribes with a valid culture. While Latins still rarely married North Americans in films of this period, they fraternized freely and openly. By the end of the war, the Latin had become a familiar film fixture, portrayed as basically equal to white Yankees, and only slightly different in culture.

The magnitude of this quantum leap in stereotypes pardons Hollywood's occasional excesses in the realm of the musical. For, at the same time, blacks remained almost entirely separated from whites in the films of this period. All-black musicals (*Stormy Weather* [20th, 1943], *Cabin in the Sky* [MGM, 1943]) were commonplace in this era, and should a musical scene with blacks be included in a film concerning whites, it was usually separated from the rest of the activity so it might be conveniently snipped by Southern censors.[36] Thus, while blacks and other minorities remained filmic pariahs, the Latins suddenly became the "Good Neighbors" next door.

THE FILMS AND THE STARS

Carmen Miranda and *The Gang's All Here*

Carmen Miranda best represented the extravagant catering to Latin American audiences during the war years. While the Rockefeller Committee members sought a Miss Pan-Americana like the Virgin Mary, they unexpectedly found the sensual Miss Miranda. She differed from every movie musical star that Holly-wood had yet discovered. Her costume was a combination of native Bahian dress and a designer's nightmare. With bare legs and midriff, she wore sweeping half-open skirts and tons of color-ful costume jewelry. She introduced the turban to the American scene, and topped it with the fruits of her native Brazil. This exaggerated Latin spectacle appeared atop five-inch platform shoes, which she claimed to have invented herself. "They come about because I like big men," the five-foot-two-inch star ex-plained. "When I dance with big men I can't see over their shoulders. Maybe they flirt with other girl. So I tell shoemaker to build up my shoes."[37]

Carmen Miranda, born Maria Do Carmo Da Cunha, was born in Lisbon and moved to Rio de Janeiro, Brazil, when she was three months old. After finishing her studies in a convent school, she worked in a department store as a model and creator of hats. Actually, she spent more time singing for the other models than engaging in store business.

A guitarist, Josue de Barros, accidentally overheard her singing at the store and arranged her first job on radio. She chose a new name, Carmen Miranda, because her father, a wealthy importer, believed entertainers were vile creatures of the lowest social status. Carmen recalled: "My father used to buy my discs and not know they were mine. He would say to me, 'You know, this Carmen Miranda, she's very good. Everybody talks about her.' I used to sit so quietly and say, 'Yes, Papa,' and inside I would die."

Finally, she was determined to tell her parents. "And, oooh, it was like fireworks. I had a big fight with my father, the neighbors would not look at me, and my boyfriend wanted his ring back. O.K., so I returned the ring, and I snubbed the neighbors. But with my father it turned out fine. I showed him I was a lady."

Lee Shubert discovered her in a Rio nightclub and brought her to Broadway for the World's Fair musical, *Streets of Paris* (1939). She ignored the title and sang "Sous Samerican Why" ("South American Way") and electrified Broadway audiences.

One critic wrote of her premiere: "Her face is too heavy to be beautiful, her figure is nothing to write home about, and she sings in a foreign language. Yet she is the biggest theatrical sensation of the year."

Twentieth Century–Fox brought her to Hollywood and almost single-handedly she spawned the studio's South American cycle (*Down Argentine Way, Weekend in Havana* [1941], *That Night in Rio* [1941], *The Gang's All Here* [1943]). When she arrived in Hollywood, she rented a group of three houses in Beverly Hills. She, her mother, two sisters, and two brothers lived in one; the six Brazilian band members lived in the second; and "some people I feel sorree for" lived in the third. In Hollywood, her home became known as the "Second Brazilian Embassy." Octavio Tavora, Brazilian Consulate attache in Hollywood, noted, "Everybody who came from Brazil wanted to visit her. Carmen was the Mary Pickford of Hollywood. She was in everybody's heart."

After each film her popularity grew, and she performed more and was given more songs and dialogue. The studio supposedly encouraged her to learn English on a very interesting fiscal basis. Fox studios promised her fifty cents for each bona fide and usable word that she added to her vocabulary. By the end of her first summer, Miranda acquired four hundred new words and a raise in salary of two hundred dollars. Despite this profitable method of learning English, Miranda's manhandling of the language won her countless admirers. She explained, "I know p'raps one hondred words—pretty good for Sous American girl, no? Best I know ten English words: MEN, MEN, MEN, MEN, and MONEE, MONEE, MONEE, MONEE, MONEE, MONEE."

Mack Gordon and Harry Warren became her official composers. Although supervised by Gilberto Souto, who provided Portuguese lyrics and watched for linguistic errors, Gordon and Warren provided the inspiration for the songs of Fox's South American cycle. Gordon vouched for the authenticity of his songs. After *Weekend in Havana*, he explained, "I feel confident of turning out a good job—I've been smoking Havana cigars for fifteen years!" He received similar inspiration for other Miranda films: "When we wrote the songs for *That Night In Rio,* we went to Monterey and took an isolated cottage on the bay there. You see, Rio is also on a bay."[38]

Her most fondly remembered film, *The Gang's All Here,* combined the talents of the queen of comic excess with the king— Busby Berkeley—and produced a bizarre display of inter-American unity. The film opens on a half-lit floating face, reminiscent of the "Lullaby of Broadway" number from *Goldiggers of 1935.* Suddenly, the camera shifts to a nightclub stage where a model of the S.S. *Brazil* is docking and unloading the major products of its country: coffee, bananas, strawberries, and then Carmen Miranda. Her hat, naturally, contains Brazil's chief exports. The nightclub host, Phil Baker, proclaims: "Well, there's your Good Neighbor Policy!" Miranda responds by teaching everyone the "Uncle Sam-ba," a dance combining elements of both North and South American rhythms.

The rest of the film, a standard love plot with Alice Faye and James Ellison, pales in comparison with Miranda's big number, the exotic "Girl in the Tutti-Frutti Hat." Carmen Miranda, drawn on a cart driven by golden oxen, arrives on a desert island laden with palm trees. The island's natives, beautiful women with six-foot bananas as hats, begin their dance. Others, carrying strawberries between their legs, lie on the floor in a typical Busby Berkeley star formation. The bananas then descend into the strawberries' midst in a sensuous slow motion rape. The banana laden natives eventually fall asleep, and Carmen Miranda leaves the stage of the most erotic production number of the 1940s.

Carmen Miranda was not alone in this exaltation of "hot-blooded" Latin women. The early 1940s also saw the flowering of the career of Lupe Velez, also known as the "Mexican Spitfire."

Lupe Velez as *Mexican Spitfire*

> Oh, yes, my deah, Lupe Velez. A very noisy young person.
>
> Mrs. William J. Locke in *Photoplay*

Even at the tender age of twelve, Lupe had sex
appeal, and no race is as quick to recognize this
trait as the Mexican.

Katherine Albert in *Photoplay*

Dolores Del Rio internalized her passions and emotions. Lupe
Velez followed shortly thereafter and opened the floodgates.
When she was young her father noted that she was "full of
pep." "No dear," replied her mother, "My Lupe is full of hell."
Lupe retained that hellish quality throughout her seventeen-year
Hollywood career, and her exuberant sexuality dwarfed all Latin
competitors. She became the "Hot Baby of Hollywood" and
"The Mexican Spitfire." Like Carmen Miranda, she had an aggres-
sive, almost mannish quality, which drove her co-stars mad in her
films about the hot-blooded Latin women.

She arrived in Hollywood knowing only a few words of English
(*chocolate malted milk, strawberry ice cream,* and *hell*). Soon
afterward, Harry Rapf, who discovered Joan Crawford dancing at
the Winter Garden Theater, also spotted Lupe in a chorus line.
A screen test led to a role with Douglas Fairbanks in *The Gaucho*
in 1927.

The plot of *The Gaucho* hardly seemed like an auspicious
start for the young Lupe. Mordaunt Hall described the story as
follows: "The Gaucho, the leader of a daredevil band, sustains a
cut on his hand after a skittish struggle with a somewhat charming young termagant (Lupe Velez). He is attacked by a victim of
the "black doom" (leprosy), and soon discovers that he himself
is a victim of the dreaded disease. He has no feeling in the hand
and it turns black. A holy theme, introduced in the prologue,
gives the Gaucho his opportunity to pray at a shrine and subse-
quently he is rid of the 'black doom.'"[39]

Lupe's performance made quite an impression. She slapped
Fairbanks with such vehemence in the film that one woman in
the opening night audience commented, "Well, now, there is a
snappy little customer." *The Saturday Evening Post* also noted
her aggressive attitude: "In that picture she had the manner of
a lady who will start a fight at any time the gentleman wishes — a

system to which she still adheres. Her religion tells her that life should consist of fighting and loving in equal parts, and anybody who is doing neither is dead and isn't aware of it."[40] *The Gaucho* led to a series of co-starring roles throughout the 1930s, and the film titles indicate the nature of Lupe's screen image: *Tiger Rose* (Par, 1929), *Hell Harbor* (Par, 1930), *The Storm* (Par, 1930), *Half-Naked Truth* (RKO, 1932), *Hot Pepper* (1933), and *Strictly Dynamite* (1934).

While Lupe's hells and damns shocked Hollywood wags, she also attracted a young and handsome Gary Cooper after they performed together in *The Wolf Song* (1929). Lupe adored the tall and silent star: "I love Garee so much that if he say to me, 'Lupe, I need your eyes,' I would take my two thumbs and gouge them out and give them to him. I only tell that to my friends. With other people I do not talk about Garee and how much I love him."

While she loved Cooper, and consorted with Ronald Colman and Ricardo Cortez, she married the Tarzan of the screen, Johnny Weissmuller in 1933. She carried her tempestuous screen life into the home and a stormy marriage resulted. When divorced in 1938, Lupe commented, "Marriage—eet stinks!"

While Lupe remained the sultry temptress during the thirties, she came into her own with the *Mexican Spitfire* series at RKO during the war years, which revived her sagging career. In the attempt to court Latin audiences, Lupe retained the furor of her earlier screen performances, but she toned down the raw sensuality.

In *Mexican Spitfire* (1939), the second of the series, Lupe portrays a married woman, Mrs. Carmelita Lindsay. The Lindsay family is upset because the son Dennis has jilted Elizabeth, a fine woman of Puritan stock, in order to marry that "Mexican Wildcat." Elizabeth and Dennis's mother are determined to break up the marriage by showing Dennis that Lupe is unrefined and lacks breeding.

In an abrupt change from her earlier films, Lupe is shown as the heroine who wishes to remain married to her Dennis. After a complicated plot concerning two cases of mistaken identity, Dennis realizes that it is Lupe whom he really loves.

Despite the toning down of Lupe's personality, she still retained the one trait that endeared her to American film audiences — her ability to fracture the English language beyond recognition. For example, when she complains that she is no good for Dennis, she laments, "I am just a gall stone around his neck." Her exchanges with Leon Errol, in the double role of Lord Epping and Uncle Matt, are filled with bizarre errors:

LEON: You look very nice and fresh.
LUPE: I am fresh, thank you.

Or:

LEON: Do you have a husband? I am footloose.
LUPE: I have a foot loose, too.

Mexican Spitfire became a quick success with critics and audiences alike, and RKO rushed out a string of sequels, each unfortunately, less interesting than the one before. *Mexican Spitfire* was followed by *Mexican Spitfire Out West* (1940), *Mexican Spitfire's Baby* (1941), *Mexican Spitfire at Sea* (1941), *Mexican Spitfire Sees a Ghost* (1942), *Mexican Spitfire's Elephant* (1942), and *Mexican Spitfire's Blessed Event* (1943).

The last title of the series was strangely prophetic. At age thirty-four, Lupe Velez, five months pregnant, took an overdose of sleeping pills in her Hollywood mansion. She left the following note to Harold Ramond, a little known French actor, with whom she had quarreled a few days earlier: "May God forgive you and forgive me too. But I prefer to take my life away and my baby's before I bring him into the world with shame or kill him. How could you, Harold, fake such great love for me and my baby when all the time you didn't want us. I see no other way out for me. So good bye and good luck to you. Love, Lupe."[41]

NOTES

1. Quoted in Bryce Wood, *The Making of the Good Neighbor Policy* (New York, 1961), pp. 130–131.

2. For a history of this office, see Donald W. Rowland, comp., *History of the Office of the Coordinator of Inter-American Affairs* (Washington, D.C., 1947).

3. *Film Daily Year Book of Motion Pictures* (1943), p. 47.

4. *Variety,* April 2, 1941.

5. Orson Welles's *It's All True* (1942), a joint venture with RKO, was one of the Division's most renowned failures. See Joseph McBride, *Orson Welles* (New York, 1973).

6. *Motion Picture Herald,* January 10, 1942.

7. *Politics,* July, 1945, p. 211.

8. Ibid.

9. *Motion Picture Herald,* April 11, 1942.

10. *Variety,* February 19, 1941.

11. Ibid., June 25, 1941.

12. For an explanation of this practice, see *The Nation,* February 15, 1941, p. 193.

13. *Newsweek,* July 22, 1940, p. 12.

14. *Moving Picture Screen and Radio Propaganda,* Subcommittee of the Committee on Interstate Commerce, September 23, 1941 ff., p. 338.

15. *Variety,* November 6, 1940.

16. Ibid., March 20, 1940.

17. Quoted in Ted Sennett, *Warner Brothers Presents* (New York, 1971), p. 280.

18. *New York Times,* April 30, 1939, IX, 5.

19. Ibid., April 23, 1939, X, 4. The other writers were John Huston and Wolfgang Reinhardt.

20. Jerome Lawrence, *The Life and Times of Paul Muni* (New York, 1974).

21. *New York Times,* July 2, 1939, X.

22. *Variety,* December 27, 1939.

23. *Time,* November 9, 1942.

24. See Tony Thomas and Jim Terry, *The Busby Berkeley Book* (New York, 1973), pp. 152–154.

25. *Variety,* October 9, 1940.

26. Ibid., October 8, 1941.

27. Ibid., June 4, 1941.

28. Ibid., November 6, 1940.

29. *O Imparcial* (Rio de Janeiro, Brazil), August 22, 1940.

30. *Variety,* November 6, 1940, p. 3.

31. *Sintonia* (Buenos Aires, Argentina), June 11, 1941.

32. *Variety,* June 25, 1941, pp. 3, 34.

33. Ibid., December 19, 1945.

34. Ibid.

35. Ibid., February 27, 1946.

36. See Donald Bogle, *Toms, Coons, Mulattoes, Mammies and Bucks* (New York, 1973), Ch. 5.

37. *New York Post,* November 30, 1955, for this quotation and those in the following paragraphs.

38. *Etude* (October, 1941).

39. *New York Times,* November 22, 1927.

40. *Saturday Evening Post,* January 2, 1932.

41. See David Zinman, *Saturday Afternoon at the Bijou* (New York, 1973), p. 426.

5

A RESPONSE ON FILM

THE LATIN AMERICAN FILM INDUSTRY TO 1950

Latin Americans had a unique advantage in their continuing battle with North American film makers. As the century progressed, Latins realized that they had the skills, technology, and talent to make their *own* motion pictures. These new films at first were unable to compare with Hollywood product, but, by the war years, Latin American films were beginning to compete with American productions. Part of the success of these South American motion pictures can be attributed to their avoidance of the standard Latin stereotypes so common in Hollywood films.

Perhaps the biggest surprise of the World War II period was the Argentine film *Petróleo* (Oil [1941]). While Hollywood was producing *Argentine Nights* and *They Met in Argentina,* which played to empty houses in Buenos Aires, *Petróleo* attracted capacity audiences for over a year. This film presented Latins as they had never been seen in North American films. *Petróleo's* chief villain is a suave North American "imperialist" (Sebastián Chiola), who arrives in Argentina to con the natives out of their oil wells. An oil man's daughter and an Argentine agent combine forces to outwit the American. The result, as one critic explained, marked the "triumph of Latin virtue over Yankee greed."[1] The *New Republic* saw this experience as a means of teaching Hollywood that "Latin Americans should be treated as equals and not as a sub-race with amusing foibles."[2]

The production of such films as *Petróleo* was not sudden or surprising, since the Latin American cinema had developed alongside the American and European industry. The birth of the Brazilian cinema, for example, hearkened back to the nineteenth century. In 1895, Louis Lumière exhibited the first motion pictures in Brazil, and two years later, the Brazilian Oswaldo Coutinho de Faria showed a film in Paris entitled *O Canto de Carlos V* (The Song of Charles V). By 1910, Paulo Beneditti, an Italian immigrant, produced a primitive sound film, *Um Transformista Original* (An Original Imposter), within the country. Early films both copied European and Hollywood originals, as well as examined Brazilian reality in such documentary films as *Guaraní* (1911), a study of the primitive Indians of the country's unsettled regions.

The majority of the other South American countries did not begin experimentation with the cinema until the present century. Often, the first films were made by immigrants who had first experienced the new art form in Europe. Mario Gallo, an Italian, made the first Argentine movie in 1908, *El Fusilamiento de Dorrego* (The Execution of Dorrego), a study of the Argentine independence movement. Most of the early Argentine films were historical studies or examinations of national character types. An analysis of the life of the gaucho (*Nobleza Gaucha*), directed by Eduardo Martínez and Ernesto Gunche in 1915, was one of the most popular of the early silent films, and it opened the eyes of entrepreneurs who saw the potentialities of the new medium.

One other classic Argentine film deserves mention. *La Loba* (The She-Wolf) appeared in 1917 and featured Carlos Gardel, a future singing idol of South America. Rudolph Valentino had seen Gardel on film and on stage, and reportedly his own interpretation of the Latin Lover owes a debt to this Argentine tango star.

The Mexicans began film-making rather late. A young engineering student, Salvador Toscano Barragán, discovered the new cinematographic apparatus while leafing through the French magazine *La Nature*. He borrowed 2,500 francs and brought the projector to Mexico City. By 1899, Toscano had nine nickelodeon theaters in Mexico, and he introduced his fellow citizens to the films of Lumière, Edison, and Méliès. The first full-length Mexican films were not produced until 1906. These early films assumed a documentary form as their titles indicate: *The Growing of Maguey* (1909), *A Day at Xochimilco* (1909), *The Bullfight* (1909), and the *Centennial Celebration* (1910). The first films with a plot were initiated in 1910. Many, like *El Grito de Dolores* (The Cry of Dolores [1910]), assumed a historical tone.[3]

The advent of sound took Latin Americans by surprise as much as the Depression did in the 1930s. Lacking the technology to counter Hollywood sound films, South America produced little of note during this period. This fact is generally agreed upon by Latin critics. Carlos Ossa Coo, author of a history of Chilean film, subtitles his chapter on the sound film "Very Little To Remember."[4] Florentino Barbosa e Silva, a Brazilian, remarked: "The advent of talking pictures was not much of a stimulus to the Brazilian movie industry, since the public passed up local films in favor of the foreign variety."[5]

Despite the lack of merit in many of these early motion pictures, a sound film industry was growing in both Mexico and Argentina.

World War II supplied the impetus to the Latin American industry that it sorely needed. In 1936, 85 percent of the Latin American films were supplied by Hollywood; by 1939, only 70 percent were of North American origin. The decrease in Hollywood films was partly the result of increased competition from Britain, Spain, France, and Germany. With the coming of the war, European film shipments to South America were quite infrequent. As a result, the Argentine and Mexican film industries expanded in order to fill the gap. In 1936, Argentina produced only twenty films each year, and, five years later, the figure had tripled. *Petróleo* is a product of this period of the revival of the flagging Argentine film industry.

The end of the war should have reversed the situation but the opposite occurred. On one hand, Latin audiences began to appreciate domestic films and their national stars. A snobbery that had viewed the local film product as inferior began to disappear.

Also contributing to the decline in North American dominence in a formerly captive market were the first cries of "cultural imperialism." This complaint differed from previous Latin criticism of American films that presented derogatory stereotypes of national character types. This new charge attacked all American films as bearers of an alien ideology and philosophy of life. A Chilean critic, referring to the "Doris Day Syndrome," asked whether the immaculate kitchens, the beautiful clothes, the luxurious ranch homes, and the sly questions of retaining one's virginity have any meaning in a developing country. He argued that the national reality would be of greater importance to a Chilean citizen.[6]

Martínez Prayva, head of the Argentine censorship office, echoed these comments in an interview in *La Época*, a leading Argentine newspaper: "Motion pictures are today the principle instrument of propaganda, and the North Americans are taking advantage of it to continue secretly spreading their ideology. We must safeguard our Argentine autonomy."[7]

While questions of cultural imperialism may have paved the way for a hostile attitude toward Hollywood films, the real crunch came with the "blocked funds" problem. The Office of International Trade of the Department of Commerce explained:

United States' motion pictures in the foreign markets of the world are now going through the most critical period in the history of the industry. This situation is by no means a result of the quality of United States pictures being sent abroad, but is the direct result of legislative barriers and trade restrictions imposed by most countries of the world on the distribution and exhibition of United States films. Our pictures are still preferred by movie-goers in most foreign markets, but the shortage of dollar exchange, resulting in frozen film earnings in a number of countries, screen quotas, high import duties, censorship regulations, and similar restrictions have caused the industry to view the future position of United States films on the foreign market with grave concern. It is conceivable that should the trend in this direction continue, U.S. films may be completely withdrawn from some foreign screens.

The most critical factor for the Latin American market was the "dollar shortage." When priorities are set in a society with scarce amounts of foreign capital, the importation of films is usually at the bottom of the list. Argentina offered the most difficulty to American distributors, granting import permits only if no foreign exchange was involved. The importation of American films was stopped on March 10, 1949, until the government would be on a stable financial footing.

In order to stem the desire for North American films, certain countries passed legislation designed to promote the local industry. Argentine theaters had to show a domestic film at least one week every month, and at least one local newsreel or documentary had to be included in the performance. By 1953, this protective law was changed to a requirement that 50 percent of all films shown should be of domestic origin. Thus, while the dollar shortage upset Hollywood producers, it had unintentionally beneficial effects for the Latin American film industry. Through the process of import-substitution, the inability to purchase the North American product led to an increase in quantity and quality of the local film product.

Despite this considerable protective legislation, it was not possible to change audience taste overnight. American and European films still remained the most successful at the box office and the most publicized in the press. In 1953, the films breaking the million peso mark in Argentina were *Detective Story* (U.S.), *Don Camilo* (Italian), *An American in Paris* (U.S.), *The Great Caruso* (U.S.), and *The Bicycle Thief* (Italian). Two Argentine films also surpassed the million peso goal: *La Casa Grande* (The Big House) and *La Mujer de las Camelias* (Camille).

As a result of the continuing popularity of the American films, several nations attempted to copy the elements that made Hollywood films so successful. This practice became most frequent in Brazil where the *chanchadas* dominated the screen. The Atlântida Company was formed in Rio in 1943 with the hope of contributing to the development of the Brazilian cinema, but it was unable to compete with American films. As a result, it turned to the *chanchada,* cheap musical comedies, wholly lacking in plot and with a strong emphasis on the music of Brazil.

On one hand, the *chanchada* led to resentment among intellectual circles, which saw these films as an attempt to pander to the lowest levels of taste. Indeed, interviews with the founders of the *Cinema Nôvo,* the Brazilian New Cinema movement, reveal that the first attempts at political film-making were a response to these imitations of the Hollywood product.

One critic, however, Alex Viany, found some value in the *chanchadas:*

The contributions of the *chanchadas* is not entirely negative. By attracting a popular audience to the cinema, they assembled the first devoted audience Brazilian films ever had. Since these films had to be accessible, they abandoned the pompous language usually associated with expensive productions: The *chanchadas* set out to capture the everyday language of the people. The success of the *chanchadas* helped raise the output of Brazilian films to almost three hundred in the fifties, and did for the Brazilian cinema what the primitive chase comedies did for the cinema of England, France, and America.[8]

Thus, in the 1950s, the Latin American cinema blossomed in Argentina and Brazil. In Mexico film production reached its apex. An average of one hundred films per year was produced during this decade. Thus, the skill was present for a collective response to the advance of the North American cinema in South America. The cinematic attack against the Hollywood film developed in the early 1950s, as younger film makers sought to develop a "new cinema," a film of meaning to the people of the Third World.

NOTES

1. *Time*, February 10, 1941, p. 70.
2. *New Republic*, February 15, 1941.
3. Emilio García Riera, *El Cine Mexicano* (Mexico City, 1963), pp. 9–10.
4. Carlos Ossa Coo, *Historia del cine chileno* (Santiago, 1971), pp. 31–41.
5. "On the Brazilian Cinema," *Américas*, 5 (June, 1953), 13–16. See also Jaime Potenze, "Argentine Movies," ibid., 6 (August, 1954), 20–23.
6. See Ariel Dorfman and Armand Mattelart, *Para leer al pato Donald: Comunicación de masa y colonialismo* (Buenos Aires, Argentina, 1972), chap. 1.
7. *New York Times*, February 6, 1948.
8. "The Old and the New in Brazilian Cinema," *Drama Review*, 14 (Winter, 1970), 142.

6

POSTWAR REALISM AND THE LATIN IMAGE

NEW PERSPECTIVES
1945–1960

As the war ended, Hollywood lost its extravagant and obsessive interest in Latin America. A calmer atmosphere pervaded postwar films concerning our neighbors to the south. Even Carmen Miranda, the Brazilian Bombshell, lost the position of prominence that she had achieved at Twentieth Century–Fox. After the war she shuffled from studio to studio in second-rate comedies and musicals like *Copacabana* (UA, 1947), *Scared Stiff* (Par, 1953), and *A Date with Judy* (MGM, 1948). The Latin exuberance was stilled as Hollywood avoided the musical stereotypes so common during World War II and looked to the dilemma of the Latin in North American society.

The film that best encapsulates Hollywood's abrupt change in attitude is *A Medal For Benny* (Par, 1945), based on a story by John Steinbeck. Benny never appears in the film. He is awarded a posthumous Congressional Medal of Honor for "killing one hundred Japs," and the townspeople of Pantera, California, have a hero on their hands. Before the war, the citizens of Pantera had ignored Benny. The only notice of his existence can be found in the jail records. Prone to drunkenness and violent outbursts, Benny was often arrested for disorderly conduct. In desperation, the city fathers finally booted the obstreperous youth out of town.

The mayor and the town council are eager to forget this fact. Suddenly the former troublemaker becomes a hero, and, just as suddenly, the town begins to take notice of its Mexican-American minority. Charlie (J. Carroll Naish), Benny's father, has repeatedly asked for a loan from the bank president in order to pay off the mortgage on his humble home. Repeatedly, he had been refused. As soon as the news of Benny's medal has been received in Pantera, the bank president escorts Charlie into his office and grants the long-awaited loan.

This sudden interest in Charlie and the other Mexican-Americans of the town is based not on social justice but on mere greed. The town is eager to exploit its newfound hero in hopes that a celebration will draw tourists, business, and investment to Pantera. Benny's role is similar to that of Eddie Bracken in *Hail the Conquering Hero* (Par, 1944) directed by Preston Sturges. Bracken is a false hero whom the city fathers desire as mayor since they can easily manipulate him. The deceased Benny is exploited in a similar fashion.

Suddenly, Old Charlie is described as "a member of one of the best families in the town" by the bank president. "Only this afternoon, he was doing business in my bank," he explains. Charlie's friends, who understand the true nature of this business, look on with horror and disdain. "Is he *loco*?" someone asks. Charlie is moved from his ramshackle hut to a palatial mansion. A photographer arrives:

PHOTOGRAPHER: Look at this land and smile. Pretend your ancestors owned it.

CHARLIE: But they did!

Charlie finally realizes that he is perpetuating a falsehood by living in this beautiful home. The pleas of the Chamber of Commerce ("You get the glory and we get the gravy") are to no avail and Charlie returns to his home late one night.

On the day of the award ceremony Charlie is nowhere to be found. The mayor and a five-star general drive to the shantytown to search for him. "You can't go there," says the mayor, "it's just a lot of shacks." "Some mighty fine Americans have come out of shacks," explains the general.

Charlie is given his son's Medal of Honor on his own doorstep. He explains to a radio audience that "Benny's house doesn't matter, because the country must depend on all kinds of people." Charlie is vindicated and the townspeople appear foolish as the film ends.

This film is unusual in many respects. Appearing at the end of the war, *A Medal for Benny* avoided the Hollywood extravaganza approach to the life of the Mexican-American. The first half of the film is a straightforward examination of the lives of the "paisanos"—defined by the title card as "a simple, friendly people who were the original settlers of California." The loves, family relationships, occupations, and social life of these citizens are explored in the film. Joe Morales (Arturo de Cordova) experiences a love life which Johnny Ramírez (*Bordertown*) lacked in the 1930s. Here he courts a woman (Dorothy Lamour) and by the end of the film wins her hand. At last, home and family are as revered as in a film with North American protagonists.

Additionally, the Mexican-American in *A Medal For Benny* is no longer the butt of the jokes, nor is he depicted as an evil character. For the first time the Anglo citizens become the villains. The leading members of the town are seen as foolish, greedy, selfish, and intolerant. The Chicanos here display the admirable traits which their white brethren seem to lack.

The attitude of the citizens of Pantera is in many ways symbolic of Hollywood's attitude toward Latin America. During the war, as European markets declined, the film industry was eager to woo Latin American film dollars and exploit native talent. As soon as the war ended and former film markets reopened, Hollywood lost interest in its Good Neighbor Policy and abandoned the Latin American extravaganzas of the wartime period.

Yet, despite the reorientation of film markets toward Europe, Hollywood had not forgotten what it had learned during the war. By 1949, the twenty Latin American republics represented almost one-fifth of the total foreign markets for American films. Less than 10 percent of the world population at this time furnished roughly 20 percent of foreign earned film royalties. While Hollywood may have lost interest in actively wooing this sizable segment of the world film audience, film producers tried not to offend or diminish it either. Memories of a burned-down Argentine theater after a showing of *Argentine Nights* as well as audience riots in Latin America forced Hollywood to realize that they could no longer win foreign audiences if they presented stereotyped or derogatory versions of the Latin character.

Hollywood's desire not to antagonize South American audiences led the Motion Picture Association of America to establish an International Information Center in Los Angeles. This advisory board hoped

first . . . to effect the deletion from motion pictures of any elements which might reasonably be expected to offend the sensitivities of foreign peoples (and) second . . . to include in motion pictures elements that may be regarded with pleasure and approbation by foreign peoples. Its third purpose is to attempt to prevent any distorted presentation of the Ameridan way of life in such a fashion that foreign audiences might draw generalized conclusions about this country.[1]

The MPAA employed two Latin American specialists—one Cuban and one North American—to assist screenwriters, directors, and producers in the preparation of scripts dealing with Latin American characters. These experts hoped to avoid any anger on the part of Latin American audiences by the elimination of derogatory Latin images in American films. The Cuban specialist offered an example of the advisory procedure:

I was brought a script which included an offensive Mexican character "El Sombre," considered "the most notorious outlaw in the old West," and his henchmen, a group of American Indians. During two conferences with the producer, I told him that to portray the only Mexican in the story as a bandit and a killer would obviously offend Mexico. After a discussion of the problem, he readily accepted my suggestion to change the nationality of the outlaw, disguise him as a Mexican and establish at the end his American nationality. To avoid offending the sensibilities of American Indians, all but one of the Indian bandits were to be eliminated.

While this advisory process attempted to eliminate images of Mexicans as rapacious bandits, it also tried to strengthen the stock portrayals of Mexican peasants as country bumpkins. This description of "Manuel Ortiz, a Mexican farmworker" was approved and viewed favorably by both of these consultants:

As suggested, he did not wear "Hollywood Mexican costumes," but dressed like an American farmer; the tiresome and excessive use of the word señor was reduced to a minimum; he did not speak offensive broken English or appear servile; nor was he treated as an inferior by the American characters. At no time was there any hint of comedy due to Ortiz' Mexican nationality. The fact that both producers were most cooperative and that the director had a deep understanding, knowledge, and affection for Mexico and its people, is clearly demonstrated in this charming and human portrayal of a Mexican character represented in an objectionable manner in the original script.[2]

Not all unfavorable views of the Latin were eliminated in this reasonable and pacific manner. The Department of the Interior in Mexico seized all film shot by John Huston for the *Treasure of Sierra Madre* (WB, 1948) in Tampico. Mayor Fernando San Pedro prohibited the Warner Brothers crew from filming scenes at the Liberty Plaza and old parts of the city in which "drunks, ragged, dirty beggars, and others astride gaunt burros were depicted by the actors." Huston protested that he was portraying Tampico in 1925, not the Mexico of today, but it was to no avail. As a result, the bordertown sequences were considerably cleaned up to satisfy the Mexican authorities.[3]

Thus, in one way or another, derogatory images of the Latin American began to disappear. Even Don Siegel's minor crime drama, *The Big Steal* (RKO, 1949), reveals a stunning reversal in the portrayal of the Mexican. Here the Americans are portrayed as greedy, spoiled, and evil. Jane Greer explains to Robert Mitchum that "it's people like you who make the Mexicans contemptuous of tourists." For a change, the Mexicans are permitted the luxury of making fun of the Americans:

> First Mexican: Is he crazy?
> Second Mexican: No, he is an American.
> First Mexican: Oh, that explains it.

As the film progresses, the American protagonists learn more and more about their Mexican neighbors. At first, Robert Mitchum plays fast and loose with the Spanish language, saying "vamoose" instead of *vamos*. Later, Mitchum learns the rules of gender:

> Mitchum (*to* Greer):   Thanks, *amigo.*
> Greer: *Amiga*— it's feminine.
> Mitchum: O.K., *amiga,* I'll stick to *chiquita*!

By the end of the film, Mitchum becomes conscious of the subtleties of the language:

> Mitchum: *Buenos noches* (Good night).
> Inspector: *Buenos tardes* (It's good afternoon).
> Mitchum: Ay! I'm sorry, Inspector general.

For the first time in the film, he pronounces *general* correctly, using a Spanish rather than an English pronunciation.

While Robert Mitchum is learning the Spanish language, the audience is learning about a new Mexican way of life. Formerly, Mexicans had been portrayed as fulfilling menial jobs in their own economy with Americans acting as a managerial elite. In *The Big Steal,* Mexicans suddenly occupy the full spectrum of occupational ranks. Mexicans own their own shops. They are barbers, mechanics, and policemen. One policeman is a graduate of the University of California. Even the police inspector

(Ramón Novarro) becomes the hero of the film. By his quick reasoning and sharp intuition he is able to find the villains and save Mitchum and Greer from an untimely demise.

Orson Welles's *A Touch of Evil* (Univ, 1958) offers yet another Mexican-American hero, although in the person of Charlton Heston, a narcotics inspector. Unwittingly drawn into a murder plot and an attempted cover-up, Mike Vargas attacks the crime establishment in a Mexican bordertown. When a young Chicano is about to be framed for a dynamite murder of a local tycoon, Vargas also opposes the local sheriff, Hank Quinlan (Orson Welles), who despises all Mexican-Americans. Vargas conquers all, saving his American wife (!) and the young Chicano and exposing the corruption in the town of Los Robles. Quinlan, the representation of evil, is left to die beneath a lonely bridge in one of the few films that allows a Latin male to portray an enforcer of the law rather than its opponent.

While the advisory boards and the protests from the Latin American governments certainly tempered the Latin image on film, one additional factor eased the awkward situation. Coproductions between North American and Latin American film companies began to appear after World War II. As often as not, these films were shot on South American soil with Latin crews and frequently with Latin actors. Hollywood tended to supply the funding, screenwriters, directors, and stars. For the first time, Latin Americans had direct participation in the making of films destined for North American audiences. Complaints that could formerly have been voiced only after the film's completion, could now be presented during the planning process. As a result, films that were formerly praiseworthy, often became elegiac as Latin Americans of heroic proportion were created in these films.

Twentieth Century–Fox's *Way of the Gaucho* (1952), filmed in cooperation with the Argentine government, idealized the mythic hero of Argentine's past. The gaucho, an equivalent to the American cowboy, is described in the film as "a special breed of man, answering to his own laws. They have vanished, but their memory lives on in the heart of a great nation." The film becomes a historical epic of nineteenth-century Argentina. Following the classic analysis of Argentine society by Domingo Faustino Sarmiento, a former Argentine president and foremost intellectual of nineteenth-century Latin America, the film displays the fight between "civilization," represented by the way of the city, and "barbarism" represented by the way of the gaucho.[4] Although Rory Calhoun, as the gaucho Valverde, must die in the name of progress, he and his kind are envisioned as "traditional fighters for freedom" and indirectly as participants in the Argentine struggle for independence from Spain.

John Ford's *The Fugitive* (RKO, 1948) attempted a similar elegy to the Mexican people, in one of the first Mexican-American coproductions. Ford entered Mexico in 1946 with no equipment but a script, six actors, including Henry Fonda and Dolores Del Rio, a production manager, and two assistants. He depended on Mexico's new Churubusco studios, partly owned by Howard Hughes and RKO, for cameramen, sound equipment and technicians, extras, props, wardrobe, interpreters, commissary, sets, and film laboratories.

Ford's dependence on the Mexican film industry was considered novel. Whenever Hollywood had ventured over the border previously, the film companies brought everything they needed with them. Henry King's *Captain from Castile* (1947) company had arrived only briefly before Ford, but what a difference! The Fox crew included a full cast and production crew, eight freightloads of equipment, plus cooks and commissary and a refrigerator unit for preserving its Technicolor film until it could be shipped to Hollywood for processing. King planned to shoot 80 percent of the film in Mexico, while Ford desired to complete the entire film in Mexico, either in the studio or on location.

Ford was pleasantly surprised with his Mexican crew members. Evidently the Hollywood denizens had expected real-life counterparts of the lazy Mexicans they had depicted on the screen, and the bustling efficiency of the Churubusco technicians surpassed all expectations. The North Americans were also startled by the modern equipment, the ample production facilities, and the sense of cooperation the Mexican workers displayed. Unlike Hollywood, Mexican film crews were organized in an industrial union. Hence, electricians could help carpenters, who in turn could help set designers, without the crossing of jurisdictional lines. North of the border, the craft unions dictated that the electrician could only work at his own skill. The rationale for this scheme in Mexico was quite deliberate. The fledgling film industry lacked Hollywood's skilled technicians. With no barriers among the various skills needed to produce the finished film product, a worker might learn various tasks until he discovers the one for which he is best suited. For this reason, Ford's relations with his Mexican crew were surprisingly satisfying.

Yet, Churubusco was not yet Hollywood, as minor technical problems plagued the brand new studio. The bank of lights in the main building was anchored to the ceiling without any provision for lowering it. Smaller sets therefore had to be separately lit.

The crews also lacked the technical wizardry of their Hollywood brethren. One scene called for a church in the town's central plaza. Ford noted that "in Hollywood, this church would have been half-inch plaster and the cobblestones would have been composition." The Mexican solution was to reproduce the church in all its splendor, with four walls of sides of foot-thick adobe. Even the street was laid with real cobblestones cemented in mortar. While this setting no doubt lent an air of reality to the proceedings, it was not easily removed after the shooting was finished. The church and the street had to be removed with sledge hammers, a time-consuming process!

Ford's main problem in the initial days of filming was his lack of knowledge of the Spanish language. He was dependent on Emilio Fernández, one of Mexico's top directors at this time. Ford would explain his instructions softly to Fernández, who in turn would issue them in boisterous Spanish at the top of his lungs with extensive gestures and countless additions to the original instructions. Shortly thereafter, Ford began to notice that the actors and crew were beginning to call Fernández *jefe* (chief). As soon as Ford discovered the meaning of the word, he resolved to reassert his authority. One morning after Fernández had reinterpreted Ford's instructions and ordered technicians, actors, and extras into place, he shouted, "Silencio!" and then waited for Ford to whisper "Roll 'em." Ford hesitated for several lengthy minutes until his crew realized that Fernández was ultimately dependent on Ford for his final instructions. With this message clearly understood, Ford whispered, "Roll 'em." From then on the American director was known as the *jefe*.[5]

The Fugitive, based on Graham Greene's novel *The Labyrinthine Ways*, is curious in its ideology from a Mexican viewpoint. Although the film glorifies a Mexican priest (Henry Fonda), it reveals a black picture of Mexican politics and society. After the Mexican Revolution, the Constitution of 1917 limited the excessive powers the Church had acquired from Spain during the colonial period. The new charter affirmed freedom of religion, nationalized clerical property, made marriage a civil contract, and prohibited clerical participation in politics. Although the Constitution thus dictated the legal separation of church and state and the ultimate secularization of Mexican society, the majority of these new laws were not enforced in the hectic period following the revolution. In 1926, however, the regime of Plutarco Elías Calles began the implementation of these laws, and prohibited alien priests, closed religious schools, and ordered priests to register with state authorities so their political activity might be regulated. In response, the clergy went on a three-year strike, closing the churches and refusing to administer Catholic rituals. Large sectors of the peasantry supported the priests, and guerrilla activity against the government was frequent in this violent period of Mexican history.[6] Ford's film ignores the historical complications and concentrates only on the role of one priest as a victim in a corrupt society bent on eliminating all religion.

The story is timeless and biblical in form. From the moment the priest opens the door of the parish church and his shadow falls on the floor in the shape of a cross, the religious dimension of the film is apparent. Fonda is a fugitive Mexican priest. He returns to his former church, now closed, and wishes to baptize the children of the village who had been denied the sacrament. The vicious police inspector (Pedro Armendáriz), of Indian blood, is determined to punish the stubborn villagers who hide priests in their midst. He decides to take hostages and kill them if the rebel priests are not turned over to the government.

Fonda eventually escapes to another state, which is sympathetic to the clerical cause, but he has discovered his sense of mission and decides to return. His only friend, Ward Bond, a fugitive thief, eventually and unwittingly leads Fonda to his death. The image of Christ among the thieves is thus strongly emphasized in the film.

Despite Fonda's death, the film ends on a note of hope, as even the bloodthirsty inspector is unable to eradicate his Christian upbringing. As Fonda dies, the inspector makes the sign of the cross over his limp body. Ultimately, a new priest arrives in the village. As he enters the church, he is bathed in light, and the image of the cross shines brightly through the grating in the door.

Although the film adopts a dismal view of Mexican society, a Mexican is once again depicted as a hero. Fonda, initially indifferent to his fate, realizes his spiritual mission through suffering, and resolves to carry the cross of the Lord in the face of adversity.

Thus the films of the postwar world further improve the image of the Latin from the dismal view of the first thirty years of the century. Despite some stereotypical backsliding, Latin society is beginning to be understood and appreciated realistically, in a far cry from the mariachi-shaking dancers of the war years. While all of the films described reveal this changing attitude, the two classic works of the post-war period—*Viva Zapata!* and *Salt of the Earth*—consider the Mexican and the Mexican-American with heretofore unknown honesty and forthrightness.

THE FILMS AND THE STARS

Elia Kazan's *Viva Zapata!*

Elia Kazan and John Steinbeck's *Viva Zapata!* (20th, 1951), a complex film in a complex era, has been attacked by Right and Left, by Mexicans and Americans. Although Kazan first considered the idea of a film about Zapata in 1935, the planning for the production was completed before the director's controversial testimony before the House Un-American Activities Committee in 1952. As a result, the film was viewed as a political statement, rather than a "historical picture," as Kazan, Steinbeck, and Darryl Zanuck had first conceived it.

At first, Kazan considered a story of Zapata, the man: "It is human character, above all, which concerns a director, writer, producer, and it was the character of Zapata which intrigued us all. He was not a man of words and what he was had to be read in what he did. Part of our interest in the beginning lay in a certain mystery about what kind of man he really was."[7] The politics of the time, both in the United States and Mexico, shifted the focus of the film, however, to the political implications of the actions of this revolutionary leader.

Kazan first sensed this attitude in an interview with Gabriel Figueroa, head of the Mexican film technician's union. He demanded changes in the script, and argued that he would urge that the film not be made in Mexico unless the alterations were made. Kazan refused, and as he left Figueroa asked, "Suppose a Mexican company came up to Illinois to make a picture about Abraham Lincoln's life with a Mexican actor playing the lead, what would you think of that?" Kazan replied, "I think it would be great . . . I'd love to see that."[8]

What Kazan first attributed to xenophobia and anti-Yankee hysteria, later appeared to him as part of a Communist plot.

We knew that the Communists in Mexico would try to capitalize on the people's reverence for Zapata by working his figure into their propaganda—much as Communists here quote Lincoln to their purpose. We had ignored this and gone about our business, for we knew that Communists anywhere and always will try to appropriate anything to which people give allegiance—peace, prosperity, land reform, brotherhood, democracy, equality, liberty, nationalism, internationalism, free speech or whatever. We can hardly give over these things to their claim."[9]

The Mexican criticism of the film script consisted mainly of supposed historical inaccuracies. They condemned references to Zapata's Spanish blood, the colonial style of his courtship and marriage, his vanity in the matter of dress and uniform, and his initial indecision to take up arms. The issue that most stirred the Mexicans, however, was Zapata's renunciation of power when the revolution finally triumphed. Kazan viewed this fact as an act of a man of individual conscience. When Steinbeck heard this criticism, he said, "I smell the Party line." Kazan noted that both the Mexican Communists and the American Daily Worker attacked the implication that "a Communist, a totalitarian, ever refused power."[10]

Ironically, while the Left denounced Kazan and Steinbeck's Zapata, the Right refused to embrace him either. A group "long on vigilance, but short on history" told Kazan that "Zapata was a rebel, so he must have been a Communist." Kazan denied the charges, since there was no Communist Party in Mexico at that time, and explained that the character of Fernando, the man who first aided and then ultimately betrayed Zapata, was created to demonstrate "the Communist mentality." Kazan believed Fernando "typified the men who use the just grievances of the people for their own ends, who shift and twist their course, betray any friend or principle or promise to get power and keep it." This Cold War and McCarthy-era rhetoric must seem bizarre in the present day, but Kazan's jargon was quite common in show business circles.

Complicating the already confused ideology of the film is an exaggerated respect and concern for all things American, topics that were no doubt foreign to Zapata and his supporters:

FERNANDO: In the United States, the Government governs, but with the consent of the people.

PABLO: That's right!

FERNANDO: They have a President, too, but he governs with the consent of the people. Here we have a President, but no consent. Who asked us if we wanted Díaz for thirty years;[11]

Despite the hazy political structure of the film, *Viva Zapata!* became a landmark in the presentation of the Latin on the screen. While it might have been easy to present these Mexican revolutionaries as modernized representations of the rapacious Latin bandits of the silent era, Kazan gave these men and women a sensitive and sympathetic portrayal. The Mexicans are presented as intelligent human beings who seek the path of revolution only after their lands have been confiscated and there is no legal recourse.

The film begins in Mexico in 1909, as Indians from the province of Morelos seek an audience with the aging dictator Porfirio Díaz. Díaz treats the peasants as children, and they behave shyly and are reluctant to talk. They complain that their land is being taken away by the owners of the large estates. Díaz calms their fears and explains that their case must be considered in the courts of law. The peasants are unsatisfied with the response, but they humbly begin to leave. One peasant remains after the others leave. Emiliano Zapata (Marlon Brando) asks the president, "Do you know of any land suits that have been won by the country people?"

"We must have patience," Díaz replies.

"We make our tortillas out of corn, not patience," answers Zapata. As Zapata leaves, Díaz circles his name on the court petition as a man who bears watching.

Since legal means bring no relief to the peasants, they cut the wire fences that have been built by the *hacendados* around their lands. A group of vigilantes open fire on the unarmed Indians. Zapata comes to their rescue, and as the vigilantes regroup, he is forced to escape to the mountains. Here he is contacted by Fernando Aguirre (Joseph Wiseman), "the man with the typewriter," who urges Zapata to meet with Francisco Madero, the leader of the first political movement against Díaz.

At this early date, revolutionary politics is not the first thing on Zapata's mind. He is more interested in Josefa (Jean Peters), the daughter of a rich merchant. The father denies Zapata's request to marry his daughter: "I don't want to see my daughter making tortillas like a common Indian." This scene correctly portrays the anti-Indian sentiment of well-to-do Mexicans of Spanish heritage during the Porfiriato.

Meanwhile, Díaz has resigned the presidency, and Madero has come to power. He appoints Zapata as his general in the south. Only now is Zapata welcome in the house of Josefa, and the youths are given permission to marry.

Zapata meets with Madero after his wedding night. The question of utmost importance to Zapata is the return of the Indian lands. Madero claims that the land will be given back, but it must be done according to the laws. To calm Zapata, Madero offers him a ranch as a reward for his loyalty. Zapata explains that "the land I fought for was not for myself." Madero, in a parody of Díaz's words answers, "It will be taken care of in good time."

By this time, the film's ideological lines are clearly drawn. Zapata is confused as to his course of action. On the right, his peasant friend, a supporter of Madero, counsels moderation. ("He's right. This is peace. We must work by law now.") Fernando urges a more ruthless course: "If Madero doesn't give the land back, then he is an enemy too. I'm a friend to no one—and to nothing except logic. . . . This is the time for killing!"

The question is soon decided for Zapata. Madero urges the peasant armies to disband, thus leaving him and his supporters vulnerable to the machinations of General Victoriano Huerta. Huerta seizes power and Madero is shot. Zapata and his followers regroup and continue the revolutionary struggle. In the process, he has his best friend, Pablo, shot for consorting with the forces of moderation.

Zapata and Pancho Villa's armies finally march triumphantly into Mexico City. Zapata is offered the presidency. In his first day in the presidential palace, peasants arrive once again and ask to have their land returned. Zapata explains that they must wait. One stubborn peasant shouts that they have waited long enough. Zapata asks the peasant's name and then realizes that he is no different than Díaz or Madero. He decides to renounce the presidency and reject the uncompromising position of Fernando:

ZAPATA: In the name of all I fought for, I'm going.
FERNANDO: If you leave now — I won't go with you. . . .
ZAPATA: I don't expect you to. . . .
FERNANDO: Thousands of men have died to give you power and you're throwing it away.
ZAPATA: I'm taking it back where it belongs; to thousands of men. (*He stares at Fernando.*) Now I know you. No wife, no woman, no home, no field. You do not gamble, drink, no friends, no love. . . . You only destroy. . . . I guess that's your love. . . . And I'll tell you what you will do now! You will go to Obregón or Carranza! You will never change!

Zapata is finally murdered by Alvaro Obregón, with the aid of Zapata's former friend Fernando. Although Zapata is dead, his legend lives. As the film ends, the townspeople look to the mountains in the belief that their hero, Emiliano Zapata, still lives and is fighting for their revolutionary goals.

Herbert Biberman's *Salt of the Earth*

It is ironic that two of the most important films about Latin Americans during the postwar era were shown so rarely. *Viva Zapata!* did dismal business in its initial engagements, and Twentieth Century-Fox lost all enthusiasm for publicizing the film. Herbert Biberman's *Salt of the Earth* (1953) appeared on few American screens as the power of the blacklist maintained its force in Hollywood.

Whereas Kazan testified at the HUAC hearings, Biberman refused to do so. As a result, he was one of the "Hollywood Ten" who went to jail.[12] After his release he joined with blacklisted author Michael Wilson, who had won an Academy Award for the screenplay of *A Place in the Sun,* to write the script for a film concerning Chicano union activity in the zinc mines of New

Mexico. Paul Jarrico, who had been fired by RKO for his refusal to answer HUAC questions, first heard of this strike while on his vacation. Apparently the local miners had been prohibited from picketing by a Taft-Hartley injunction, so the wives assumed their positions on the picket line and continued the strike. Jarrico believed that the incident had great dramatic possibilities and suggested Wilson for the screenwriting task.

From the outset, the creators strived to correct the errors that previous generations of filmmakers had made when portraying Latins on the screen. Initially, Wilson designed the female lead for Gale Sondergaard, Biberman's wife. Suddenly Biberman was struck by the hypocrisy of this action: "We were preparing a film of the Mexican-American people. But we had selected two Anglos to play the leads! Oh, we planned to use Mexican-Americans in the small parts. But we couldn't entrust Mexican-Americans with the *important* Mexican-American roles. The Hollywood tradition! And we were carriers!"

As a result, a Mexican actress, Rosaura Revueltas, was chosen for the lead role of Esperanza. She had appeared in only three films previously in her native Mexico, but she had won national film awards for two of them. After much indecision, the newly elected president of the zinc worker's union, Juan Chacon, a man with no acting experience, was chosen as the male lead. In this fashion, Biberman avoided the standard practice of using "false" Latins for his stars, a common tradition since the beginning of the century. The same sense that led Biberman to place Latins in the lead roles also led to the most perceptive film about Mexican-Americans ever made.

Salt of the Earth is dedicated to New Mexico, "the land of the free Mexicans who inspired this film." The picturesque vistas of Southwestern American landscape are suddenly disrupted by the images of the zinc mines which ruined the beauty of this former Spanish territory. Even the original Spanish name of the town is eradicated. It is now named "Zinctown."

Esperanza (Rosaura Revueltas), wife of Ramón (Juan Chacon), a miner, narrates this story of the changing mores of a Mexican-American community after its daily life is interrupted by a lengthy and bitter strike. Esperanza is a homebody. She spends her days washing, ironing, and caring for her two children. As the film begins, she hopes that her third child will not be born into such a violent world. Her fears are reinforced as her eldest son returns home from school, bruised and battered by a gang of Anglo youths who made fun of him.

The same split between Anglos and Mexican-Americans exacerbates tensions at the local mine. The Mexican miners refuse to enter the mine alone since all Anglo workers at nearby mines labor in groups of two for safety reasons. The Anglo foreman finds the Mexicans lazy, and when he hears talk of a strike he vows that he can find other workers easily. "Who will you find," ask the miners, "scabs?" "No, Americans," replies the foreman.

As the men begin to discuss strike demands, Esperanza asks them to consider the deplorable state of sanitation in the mine-owned shantytown. Ramón ignores her: "You're only a woman; you don't know what it is like to work!" Esperanza answers, "Always the men will come first!" She retreats, crying, to her bedroom.

The women decide to form a delegation to present their demands at a strike meeting. Esperanza is shocked at this idea: "A picket line for ladies? If Ramón found me in a picket line, he'd. . . ." "Beat you?" asks another woman. A siren interrupts the women's talk. An ambulance races to the mine. A worker has been injured in a cave-in. Immediately the men refuse to return to the mine and they have a strike vote. The strike is overwhelmingly approved, 93 to 5.

The women tentatively attend the strikers' first meeting. One woman cautiously speaks up. "We should have equality at home, too. Let us form a Ladies' Auxiliary." The men laugh at this audacious thought and the motion is tabled until the next meeting. One woman shouts, "Why don't you put a sign outside? — No dogs or women allowed." Although Esperanza attends the meeting, she says nothing. "At least you didn't make a fool of yourself," Ramón comments.

At first the women stay away from the picket line. But, one

day, the elderly Mrs. Salazar, wife of a miner killed in the pits, joins the men on the line. Suddenly, the other women begin to come to make tacos and coffee for their husbands. Esperanza is allowed to join them since Ramón thinks that the other women's coffee tastes like "zinc sludge."

The local representative of the mining firm arrives and sets the tone of the entire strike. "The Mexicans are like children in many ways. Sometimes you have to humor them; sometimes you have to spank them; and sometimes you have to take their food away."

The deputies then grab Ramón and rough him up. As this occurs, Esperanza goes into labor. The police refuse to take her to a hospital so the baby must be delivered on the spot. As the baby is about to be born, Esperanza prays that it will die so it will never see this ugly world. Ramón is arrested for assault and resisting arrest as his son is born.

The strike continues and funds are rapidly being exhausted. Other unions have taken notice of the plight of these Chicanos, however, and donations to the strike fund begin to arrive. Owing to the increased correspondence from outside New Mexico, the women are moved from their coffee-making chores to an office, where they type, address, and stamp replies to these letters.

Meanwhile, the sheriff (Will Geer) arrives with word of the latest attempt of the mine-owners to break the strike. The Taft-Hartley Act is used to prohibit further picketing by the miners. The men are disconcerted; they have no solution. The women, however, present an ingenious plan. There is nothing in the injunction preventing the *wives* of the miners from picketing. Ramón is against the idea, and the question is called. The women protest because they are not allowed to vote by the union by-laws. As a result, the union leaders adjourn the meeting and call a community meeting in which the women may vote. The ladies maintain the balance of power, and the motion is carried although most of the men are opposed.

The next morning women from nearby mining camps arrive to take their place on the picket line, but Ramón forbids Esperanza to participate. As the deputies attempt to break the new picket lines, Esperanza can remain on the sidelines no longer. She hands Ramón the baby and helps her neighbors resist the forces of the law. The women beat off the deputies and sing "We Shall Not Be Moved." The women are now in charge.

Esperanza, radiant, returns home with a new sense of usefulness in this world. Ramón, however, is irate because "he had to watch the kids all day." "I've watched them every day since they've been born," Esperanza replies.

The next morning the women are given an ultimatum. They must disband the line or go to jail. They refuse and their leaders, including Esperanza, are arrested. This move is unsuccessful. First, women from nearby mines arrive and take the place of the absent leaders. Second, the jailed women protest constantly. Their incessant noise annoys the sheriff so, that he is compelled to release them.

In the interim, Ramón becomes a surrogate mother. He is forced to watch the children, iron, and wash clothes. As Ramón hangs the laundry, he realizes the importance of his wife's demands for hot running water in the town.

Esperanza is released from jail, but she is now a stronger woman. Ramón is hurt and alienated by her lack of attention and her unwillingness to resume her previous submissive role in their relationship:

> ESPERANZA: Have you learned nothing from this strike? Why are you afraid to have me at your side? Do you think that you can have dignity only if I have none?
>
> RAMÓN: You talk of dignity? After what you've been doing?
>
> ESPERANZA: Yes. I talk of dignity. The Anglo bosses look down on you, and you hate them for it. "Stay in your place, you dirty Mexican"—that's what they tell you. But why must you say to me, "Stay in your place"? Do you feel better having someone lower than you?
>
> RAMÓN: Shut up, you're talking crazy.
>
> ESPERANZA: Whose neck shall I stand on to make me feel superior? And what will I get out of it? I don't want

anything lower than I am. I'm low enough already. I
want to rise. And push everything up with me as I go.[13]

Ramón leaves for a hunting trip, although Esperanza fears that
the mine owners might try something while the men are gone.
The supervisors try their last card—they attempt to evict Ramón's
family from their home. Ramón, although miles away, remembers
Esperanza's warning. He urges his friends to return and he arrives
just in time to stop the deputies from ransacking his home.

Ramón does not resist alone. "Now we can fight together,"
he tells his wife. As hundreds of miners and their wives gather
around the Quintero home, the women begin to return household
items to the home as fast as the lawmen remove them. Eventually, so many supporters arrive that the deputies give up their
attempted eviction and the mine owners decide to negotiate.

Ramón and Esperanza are reconciled. Their married life will
now be based on equality instead of the *macho* norms Ramón
had formerly exalted. Ramón thanks Esperanza "for her dignity,"
and agrees that she was right in her opinions. "Together we can
push everything up with us as we go," explains Ramón. Esperanza
clasps Ramón's hand and they walk into their house. Her voice
is heard as the scene fades: "Then I knew we had won something
they could never take away—something that I could leave to our
children—and they, the salt of the earth, would inherit it."

NOTES

1. *Américas,* October, 1949, p. 3.

2. Ibid., p. 5.

3. *New York Times,* February 22, 1947.

4. D. F. Sarmiento, *Life in the Argentine Republic in the Days of the Tyrants*
(New York, 1868).

5. *New York Times Magazine,* March 23, 1947, p. 17.

6. Frederick C. Turner, *The Dynamic of Mexican Nationalism* (Chapel Hill,
1968), p. 139. See also Michael Wilmington, "Ford's *The Fugitive,*" *The Velvet
Light Trap,* 5 (Summer, 1972), 33–35.

7. *Saturday Review,* April 5, 1952, p. 22.
8. Michel Ciment, *Kazan on Kazan* (Viking Press, 1973), p. 90.
9. *Saturday Review,* April 5, 1972, p. 22.
10. Ibid.
11. John Steinbeck, *Viva Zapata!* (Viking Press, 1975).
12. See Stefan Kanfer, *A Journal of the Plague Years* (New York, 1973).
13. Herbert Biberman, *Salt of the Earth* (Boston, 1965), pp. 43–44.

7

EPILOGUE:
THE RETURN OF
THE GREASER

CONTEMPORARY IMAGES

Thus the story would seem to be over. In the postwar period
Hollywood's actors, writers, and directors reached newfound
heights in the sympathetic treatment of Latin Americans on
the screen. There remained problems, to be sure. A hesitancy
remained to cast Latins in major film roles. Hence Marlon
Brando portrayed Emiliano Zapata and Henry Fonda a Mexican
priest in *The Fugitive*. But even this tendency seemed to be
abating by the late 1950s, as younger stars of Latin American
heritage, such as Fernando Lamas and Ricardo Montalban,
achieved prominence on the American screen in several important roles.

Societal progress would seem to be the key, continual improvement the rule. By 1960, it appeared that Latins would be the first major minority group to achieve equality on the screen, with regard both to access to starring roles and the elimination of derogatory stereotypes. Blacks and native Americans might achieve a similar status, but they would have to wait almost another decade.

As a result of the continual improvement in the Latin American image on the screen between 1940 and 1960, the return of the "greaser" was a major and unexpected surprise. By the mid-1960s, as violence returned to the modern screen, a new villain was resurrected. Whether in the spaghetti Westerns of Sergio Leone or the films of Sam Peckinpah, the murderous, treacherous, and violent Latin American reappeared on the screen. With the new heights of filmic savagery presented on the screen during the last decade, violence by Latin bandits became excessive and widespread. Whereas during the silent era the greaser might vent his wrath on individuals or small groups, modern screen technology allows the Mexican to destroy mass portions of the population. In *Duck, You Sucker* (UA, 1972), Rod Steiger, portraying a peasant during the Mexican Revolution, is prone to throwing bombs every few minutes in order to destroy trains, munition dumps, and the like.

At the same time that the Latin is being newly chastised for his inherent violent streak, he also becomes the target of film comedy. In *Viva Max* (CUE, 1970), a disgruntled Mexican general, portrayed by Peter Ustinov, attempts to recapture the Alamo from the United States, aided by only a small troop of men. Or *Bananas* (UA, 1971) explodes the mythic stature of Latin American revolutionaries by directing Howard Cosell to cover the latest palace coup on the island of San Marcos for ABC's "Wide World of Sports." At least the ostensible object of *Bananas* is humorous with virtually everyone the brunt of Woody Allen's jokes (i.e., J. Edgar Hoover, Miss America, and Nelson Eddy and Jeanette MacDonald). *Che!* (20th, 1969) also deflates the reputation of the famed Latin American guerrilla leader, only here the goal is supposedly "objective and documentary."

The films of the modern era have thus reinstated myths about the Latin American which had remained dormant for fifteen years. At this writing, a new set of rules governing portrayals of Latin Americans seem to be in effect:

1. The Latin American is extraordinarily violent.

2. The Latin American, whether peasant, landlord, revolutionary, or whatever, is the subject of scorn or ridicule.

3. Yet, no matter how violent the Latin American, he is unable to cope with either the strength or superior technology of the North American hero.

The last rule, yet another holdover from the silent era, has been demonstrated in such recent films as *Butch Cassidy and the Sundance Kid,* wherein Robert Redford and Paul Newman manage to kill hundreds of Bolivians without the slightest personal injury. Similarly, in *Bring Me the Head of Alfredo Garcia* (Par, 1974), Warren Oates is able to assassinate a rich Mexican landowner, despite the efforts of hundreds of Mexican guards to stop him. Even when North Americans are allied with Latins, the latter seem effete and childish. *Two Mules for Sister Sara* (Univ, 1970) demonstrates that the Mexican Revolution would never have been won without the aid of Clint Eastwood.

The humorous dimensions of the Latin American have been expanded with the representation of a new and unexpected comic figure — the revolutionary. From the date of Fidel Castro's rise to power in Cuba, the bearded guerrilla has become the brunt of jokes and the object of scorn. As relationships between the United States and Central and South American countries have deteriorated during the last decade, this new comic figure has appeared more and more often in American films.

While Hollywood has nullified some twenty years of progress in the depiction of the Latin American in film, films made in South American nations portraying Latin American society sympathetically have had very little exposure in the United States. Most films of the "third cinema" remain relegated to showings at film festivals or by university film societies. Even the prestige of a film festival is no longer an assurance that these films will be seen even by a small segment of the viewing audience.

Occasionally political factors can heighten the difficulty of
viewing Latin American films, as demonstrated by the proposed
Cuban Film Festival at the Olympia Theatre in New York City
in 1972. During the premiere of Humberto Solas's *Lucia,* an anti-
Castro group released stink bombs and white mice in the theater.
This discomfort was minor compared to what occurred the
following afternoon. Representatives of the Treasury Department arrived, and confiscated the remaining films under the pro-
visions of the Trading with the Enemy Act, which requires that
all Cuban imports to the United States be licensed by the government. As a result, the festival was abruptly closed.

The promoters of the festival called the move "vindictive"
and "absurd," and the precise timing of the seizure would seem
to support charges of government harassment. First of all, advertisements for the film series had been appearing in the newspapers for months. Second, some of the films had already been
shown elsewhere without incident. The Museum of Modern Art
in New York had featured Tomás Gutiérrez Alea's *Memories of
Underdevelopment* (Cuba, 1968) in a film showcase of the works
of new directors and no attempts were made to stop that showing. Finally, the immigration department had denied all visas to
the Cuban film directors who had been invited to the festival by
American Documentary Films. Although the festival was abruptly
squelched, many of the films have achieved a limited distribution
since 1972 without similar attempts to prohibit their exhibition.
Nonetheless, films by Latin Americans which present Latins in a
favorable light have been seen by only a small segment of the
American viewing audience.[1]

What is to be done? Trade boycotts of American films and
film censorship remain an effective if localized weapon. Mexico
banned *They Came to Cordura* (Col, 1959) in 1960 because its
portrayal of Pershing's punitive expedition into Mexico was
"historically false."[2] Spain carried this method to a further
extreme. After *Behold a Pale Horse* (Col, 1964), an account of the
Spanish Civil War, offended Spanish censors, all import licenses
for Columbia pictures were denied for three years.[3] As a result,

MGM entered into negotiations with Spanish diplomats before filming Peter Shaffer's Broadway play, *Royal Hunt of the Sun,* which concerned the Spanish conquest of Peru. Spanish sources claimed that the play presented "a distorted picture of Pizarro's conquest of the Incas, depicting his men as sadistic, greedy, and power hungry."⁴ Although Spain officially denied these rumors, production of the film was delayed almost two years.

Another manner of controlling derogatory characterizations of Latins in American films comes as an unintended result of the nationalization of American film companies as occurred in both Cuba (1965) and Chile (1971). The firms were expropriated for a variety of reasons, with the dollar drain being the prime factor. Those films remaining within the country at the time of the confiscation were turned over to the domestic film distribution agencies, the Cuban Institute of Cinematographic Art and Chile Films. Thus, an unforeseen and beneficial result of these actions allowed the national governments to control the distribution of certain American films within domestic markets and eliminate any offensive films.

Yet neither of these so-called solutions attack the problem at the source in Hollywood. One of the most fruitful methods of controlling the presentation of unfavorable Latin stereotypes has been the exerting of pressure on film studios, producers, actors, and writers *before* the film is made. In this manner West Coast groups prevented the filming of *Christophe of Haiti* with Anthony Quinn, a non-black and a non-Haitian, in the title role. Showings of *Juarez* and *Bordertown* have been eliminated from late night shows on Los Angeles television stations owing to viewer complaints that the leading characters are not portrayed by actual Latins. Perhaps the most notable attempt to negotiate with the studios in order to change derogatory Latin stereotypes occurred during the filming of the television show *Chico and the Man.* Members of the Latin community of Los Angeles argued that the lead character, Chico, is a Mexican-American, whereas Freddie Prinze, the star of the show, is of both Puerto Rican and Hungarian heritage. Local Chicano groups argued that a non-Chicano should not perform in a major television role while so few Mexican-Americans were employed in the industry. These citizen organizations also challenged the lazy, shiftless character of Chico, claiming that it defamed the image of the Mexican-American. After repeated meetings with the production staff at NBC, and a continual picketing of the studios, the producers agreed to hire Chicanos in supporting roles and tone down Prinze's portrayal of the Chicano.

Unfortunately, if peaceful means fail to eliminate offensive portrayals of the Latin, violence may become a last resort. Puerto Rican groups were unable to prevent Paramount's *Badge 373* (1973) from painting a bleak picture of the Puerto Rican character. As Vincent Canby commented in his *New York Times* review: "All the evil is perpetrated by Puerto Ricans, either innocent but violent revolutionaries who run around shouting 'Puerto Rico libre,' or uninnocent but violent non-revolutionaries who manipulate them." At no time did it appear that any Puerto Rican might have a logical reason for wishing the island freed from North American domination.[5]

Soon after the film opened, a group of one hundred Puerto Ricans began to protest at the Gulf and Western Building, the home of the parent company of Paramount Pictures in New York. They argued that *Badge 373* was a "racist film," since it "denigrated the Puerto Rican community" and "vividly expresses the lack of respect for the dignity of the Puerto Rican people."[6] The protesters urged that the film be withdrawn from public viewing and that representatives of the Puerto Rican community be allowed to review future film scripts that concerned Latins.

The Puerto Rican Action Coalition ultimately met with Frank Yablans, president of Paramount, in order to press their demands. He refused to withdraw the film from circulation, noting that "it was made clear that such discussion could not go forward in an atmosphere of duress and pressure." He added that he would welcome future meeting "in a spirit of mutual respect and harmony." The Coalition's complaints remained unheeded. Shortly thereafter a small bomb exploded at one of the theaters showing *Badge 373*.[7]

It is clear that Hollywood can no longer accept portrayals of the Latin which had appeared doomed to extinction in the early 1940s. While filmmakers have at last reached a level of sensitivity heretofore unknown in its treatment of blacks and native Americans, the Latin remains the odd man out. For this reason, the section describing "The Films and the Stars" for the 1960s and 1970s resembles that of the 1920s and 1930s. All major Latin roles are portrayed by North Americans, and the South American remains an object of scorn. Instead of progress, only a vicious circle emerges.

THE FILMS AND THE STARS

> I think I know more about Che than anyone. He is basically a man who wanted to put his life in danger. He is almost like Lawrence of Arabia.
>
> > Omar Sharif in *New York Times Magazine,* December 8, 1968
>
> Che, in a way, was something like Vince Lombardi, Jesus Christ and Vince Lombardi! How's that?
>
> > Robert Loggia in *New York Times Magazine,* December 8, 1968

Che!

From the first moments of planning, *Che!* (1969) seemed destined to become a controversial film. Twentieth Century–Fox assembled a glamorous cast (Omar Sharif, Jack Palance) and supplied an ample budget for a film that was designed as an objective account of the life of Che Guevara. "Life" is the precise word, as all political considerations dropped by the wayside. The producer of the film, Sy Bartlett, commented: "We are doing purely the story of Che, the person, not the movement. We want to show what happened with the people who touched his life."[8]

Despite the desire for a personal and objective account, politics could not be eliminated. From the outset, the complex system of international relations between the United States and Latin America interfered with the creation of the filmic *Che!* The

first major decision—to shoot the film in Puerto Rico—was
dictated by political considerations. Richard Fleischer, the director, explained: "We thought about the possibilities of doing it in
Mexico, Brazil, and the Philippines—and Puerto Rico. We had to
find a place that likes Americans. That narrows it down. We
needed a location far from political upheaval. That ruled out
South America." The similar landscapes to Cuba, the inexpensive
labor costs, and government incentives clinched the deal for
Puerto Rico.[9]

At first Bartlett was reluctant to do the film, claiming that "a
picture based on Che's life could turn into a favorable propaganda platform for Communists and Communism."[10] The Zan-
ucks, then in charge at Fox studios, urged production of the film
for a variety of reasons. One publicity release claimed that "the
unwavering dedication of the Argentine doctor, whose heroic
exploits in the Cuban revolt were legion, and the ultimate hard-
ships suffered by his obdurate campaign to spread revolution
and violence throughout Latin America with his resultant failure
and death—all these were of great significance and possessed
tremendous potential for a good dramatic theme." This release
expresses the ambivalence toward Che that plagued the film
from inception to completion. Che was both a hero and a villain,
but no one seemed able to decide which personality dominated.

Darryl Zanuck expressed a more personal evaluation of the
genesis of Che!: "I wish the late Errol Flynn were alive, as he
personally participated in the last phase of the overthrow of
Batista, and was, in the early days, an intimate friend of Guevara.
Even then Che seems to have been "publicity conscious" or at
least aware of my record in producing controversial films such
as *The Grapes of Wrath, How Green Was My Valley, Gentlemen's
Agreement*, etc., and Guevara had commissioned or authorized
Errol to contact me about making a film on the birth of Castro's
Cuba."[11] Despite these general descriptions of the film's origin,
it is more than likely that the recent resurgence of Che's popularity during the antiwar movements of the late 1960s contributed
greatly to the decision to make the film.

The first film treatment was deemed unsatisfactory. Michael Wilson was called in to prepare the second draft. This in itself was a polemic move. Although Wilson had written the screenplays for such popular films as *Thousands Cheer* (MGM, 1943) and *A Place in the Sun* (Par, 1951), he was also a blacklisted member of the Hollywood Ten and author of the controversial *Salt of the Earth*. Fleischer noted that "there wasn't any trouble about Wilson as a screenwriter. That's all over now. The only trouble came from a couple of members of the board of directors at Fox. After all, the subject is controversial."[12] The final screenplay is credited to Michael Wilson, and based on the research by Sy Bartlett. Yet the final text maintains an ahistorical tone, as the following disclaimer reveals: "None of the various texts written on Che Guevara, nor his published diary penned by the revolutionary during the Bolivian episode, was utilized in the final treatment from which this screenplay was adapted." The film itself is a particular account of Che's life in Cuba and Bolivia. His life prior to his revolutionary commitment is eliminated from the film. Régis Debray, Che's ally, is cut from the film, and his girl friend Tania merely provides the subsidiary love interest. ("Debray wasn't that important. And Tania's story was just too corny," Fleischer explained.)[13]

Despite the lofty goals of the producers and screenwriters ("Twentieth Century–Fox will produce an objective, unbiased story of the fiery revolutionary"), the critics were singularly unimpressed. Vincent Canby explained in the *New York Times* that the only value of the film was "a reminder that the Old Hollywood Dream Factory still has the constitution of a goat. It can consume almost everything — including a subject as complex and abrasive as the late Cuban revolutionary — and reduce it to the consistency of strained spinach."[14]

The Che of the film is depicted as a misguided fool. He is presented in an unfavorable light due to his hatred of America and his firm support of Russian missiles on Cuban soil. When Che attempts to export the revolution to Bolivia, the film's Fidel fears that his deluded friend is losing contact with reality. In Bolivia events turn from bad to worse. Che explains to a goatherd that he has come to free him. The peasant replies: "To free me from what? Ever since you came to these mountains with your guns and your fighting my goats give no milk." Even the Bolivians wish Che would disappear. He is executed by the Bolivian army, and, in the last few moments, the United States is absolved of all guilt as "the CIA was not involved in any way."[15]

Bananas

Despite the pretensions of accuracy in *Che!*, Hollywood presented an image of the ineffectual revolutionary. The film implicitly argued that the urban and rural guerrillas are out of step with the historical realities of South America and are not viewed favorably by the masses. Woody Allen's *Bananas* (1971) continues this dissection of the revolutionary, reducing him to a comic figure interested only in personal power instead of the needs of the people who support his struggle.

Like *Che!*, *Bananas* was filmed in Puerto Rico, where Howard Cosell and the ABC "Wide World of Sports" team arrive to film the "Assassination of the Week" on the mythical island of San Marcos. Fielding Mellish (Woody Allen) becomes a political pawn in the hands of the dictator-of-the-month, General Emilio Vargas, who wishes to kill him and blame the murder on the rebel troops. Vargas hopes that his act would bring American support of his regime in the fight against the guerrillas. Esposito, the rebel leader who strangely resembles Fidel Castro, rescues Fielding from the clutches of the government forces. Fielding is eventually converted to the rebel cause and is sent on a dangerous mission to a local delicatessen to obtain one thousand corned beef sandwiches for the rebel forces.

Esposito's troops capture the capital. Once in power, however, he forgets his promises to the people of San Marcos. He declares that Swedish will be the island's new official language and that the people must change their underwear every thirty minutes and wear them on the outside of their clothes. Fielding helps remove the crazed Esposito from power and he is proclaimed president of the island.

The rebels then send Fielding to New York to gain support for the new government. The visit to New York, with Fielding wearing fatigues and a red beard, recalls Castro's last visit to the United States. Fielding's identity is accidentally revealed, and he is charged with treason. Fortunately, he is given a suspended sentence when he agrees not to move into the judge's neighborhood. By the end of the film, Fielding's flirtation with Latin America is forgotten, and he marries his girl friend, Louise Lasser, and Howard Cosell returns to cover the wedding night for ABC news.

Woody Allen skillfully exploits every long-standing myth concerning Latin American politics. The governments are seen as unstable, controlled alternately by leftist guerrillas and military dictators. The only concern in the political arena becomes the control of power. Once the presidency is achieved, all revolutionary fervor immediately vanishes. As both Cuba under Castro and Chile under Allende have demonstrated, however, this is not necessarily a truism. As a result, after *Che!* and *Bananas*, the Latin American revolutionary becomes an object of derision or laughter, a new myth for a new age.

NOTES

1. For an account of the film festival, see *Newsweek*, April 17, 1972, and Vincent Canby, "Stick Bomb Yes—Cuban Festival, No!" *New York Times*, April 2, 1972, II, 1. For an account of recent trends in Latin American film, see Ian Cameron, ed., *The Third Wave* (New York, 1968), and Octavio Getino and Fernando Solanas, "Towards a Third Cinema," *Afterimage* 3 (1971), 16–35.

2. *New York Times*, January 9, 1960.

3. Ibid., March 8, II, 9:1.

4. Ibid., April 23, 26, 1966.

5. Ibid., July 26, 1973.

6. Ibid., August 11, September 9, 1973.

7. Ibid.

8. John Leonard, "Will the Real Che Guevara Please Stand Up and Die for Our Popcorn?" *New York Times Magazine,* December 8, 1968, pp. 57 ff.

9. *New York Times,* November 12, 1968.

10. *New York Times Magazine,* February 9, 1969, p. 101.

11. Leonard, "Will the Real Che Guevara Please Stand Up?"

12. *New York Times,* November 12, 1968.

13. Ibid.

14. *New York Times,* May 30, 1969.

15. Leif Furhammar and Folke Isaksson, *Politics and Film* (New York, 1971), pp. 150–151.

BIBLIOGRAPHY

FILMOGRAPHY

The Americano (Biograph, 1916)
Bananas (United Artists, 1971)
The Big Steal (RKO Radio Pictures, 1949)
Bordertown (Warner Brothers, 1935)
Bring Me the Head of Alfredo García (United Artists, 1974)
Captain from Castile (Twentieth Century–Fox, 1947)
Che! (Twentieth Century–Fox, 1969)
Duck, You Sucker (United Artists, 1972)
Flying Down to Rio (RKO Radio Pictures, 1933)
The Fugitive (RKO Radio Pictures, 1947)
The Gang's All Here (Twentieth Century–Fox, 1943)
Girl of the Rio (RKO Radio Pictures, 1932)
Go into Your Dance (Warner Brothers, 1935)
The Good, Bad, and the Ugly (United Artists, 1967)
Hi Gaucho (RKO Radio Pictures, 1936)
In Caliente (Warner Brothers, 1935)
I Live for Love (Warner Brothers, 1935)
Juarez (Warner Brothers, 1939)
The Last Movie (Universal, 1971)
Latin Lovers (Metro-Goldwyn-Mayer, 1954)
A Medal for Benny (Paramount, 1945)
Mexican Spitfire (RKO Radio Pictures, 1939)
Pan-Americana (RKO Radio Pictures, 1945)
Rio Rita (Metro-Goldwyn-Mayer, 1941)
Salt of the Earth (Independent Production, 1953)
Sergeant York (Warner Brothers, 1941)
Springtime in the Rockies (Twentieth Century–Fox, 1940)
Thank Your Lucky Stars (Warner Brothers, 1943)
That Night in Rio (Twentieth Century–Fox, 1941)
They Met in Argentina (RKO Radio Pictures, 1941)
Three Caballeros (Disney, 1945)
Too Many Girls, (RKO Radio Pictures, 1940)
A Touch of Evil (Universal, 1958)
The Treasure of Sierra Madre (Warner Brothers, 1948)
Viva Max! (Commonwealth-United-Entertainment, 1969)
Viva Villa! (Metro-Goldwyn-Mayer, 1934)

Viva Zapata! (Twentieth Century-Fox, 1952)
Way of the Gaucho (Twentieth Century-Fox, 1952)
West Side Story (United Artists, 1961)

PERIODICALS

Américas
Etude
Filmfacts
Films in Review
O Imparcial (Rio de Janeiro)
Motion Picture Herald
Moving Picture World
Photoplay
La Prensa (Buenos Aires)
Primer Plano, revista de cine (Valparaiso, Chile)
Sintonia
Variety
The Velvet Light Trap

BOOKS AND ARTICLES

Barbosa e Silva, Florentino. "On the Brazilian Cinema," *Américas,* 5 (June, 1953), 13–16.
Bergman, Andrew. *We're in the Money.* New York, 1971.
Biberman, Herbert. *Salt of the Earth.* Boston, 1965.
Bogle, Donald. *Toms, Coons, Mulattoes, Mammies, and Bucks.* New York, 1973.
Botting, David Charles. "History of the Motion Picture in Latin America," unpub. Ph.D. dissertation, University of Chicago, 1950.
Brownlow, Kevin. *The Parade's Gone By.* New York, 1968.
Cameron, Ian, ed. *The Third Wave.* New York, 1968.
Ciment, Michel. *Kazan on Kazan.* New York, 1973.
Croce, Arlene. *The Fred Astaire and Ginger Rogers Book.* London, 1972.
de Núbila, Domingo. *Historia del cine argentino.* Buenos Aires, 1959.
Eisenstein, Sergei, and Upton Sinclair. *The Making and Unmaking of 'Que Viva Mexico'.* Bloomington, Ind., 1970.
Film Daily Year Book of Motion Pictures. Los Angeles, 1941.
Furhammar, Leif, and Folke Isaksson. *Politics and Film.* New York, 1971.
García Riera, Emilio. *Historia documental del cine mexicano.* Mexico City, 1969.
Gerbi, Antonello. *La Disputa del nuevo mundo.* Mexico City, 1960.
Gonzaga, Adhemar. *70 Anos de Cinema Brasileiro.* Rio de Janeiro, 1966.
Greenfield, Concetta Carestia. "The New South American Cinema: From Neo-Realism to Expressive Realism," *Latin American Literary Review,* I (Spring, 1973), 140–149.
Harley, John Eugene. *World Wide Influences of the Cinema: A Study of Official Censorship and the International Cultural Aspects of Motion Pictures.* Los Angeles, 1940.

Hijar, Alberto, ed. *Hacia un tercer cine.* Mexico, 1972.

Kanfer, Stefan. *A Journal of the Plague Years.* New York, 1973.

Keen, Benjamin. *The Aztec Image.* New Brunswick, 1971.

Lawrence, Jerome. *The Life and Times of Paul Muni.* New York, 1974.

Leonard, John. "Will the Real Che Guevara Please Stand Up and Die for Our Popcorn," *New York Times Magazine,* December 8, 1968, pp. 57 ff.

Loy, Jane M. "Latin America through Film: Problems and Possibilities," *Proceedings of the PCCLAS,* I (Summer, 1973), pp. 30–40.

Martínez Torres, Augusto, and Manuel Pérez Estremera. *Nuevo cine latinoamericano.* Barcelona, 1973.

Merritt, Russ. *Marquee Theatre.* Madison, Wisc., 1971.

Moving Picture Screen and Radio Propaganda. Subcommittee of the Committee on Interstate Commerce. Washington, D.C., 1942.

Ossa Coo, Carlos. *Historia del cine chileno.* Santiago, 1971.

Potenze, Jaime. "Argentine Movies," *Américas,* 6 (August, 1954), 20–23.

Ramsaye, Terry. *A Million and One Nights: A History of the Motion Picture.* New York, 1964.

Rocha Glauber. "The Old and the New in Brazilian Cinema," *Drama Review,* 14 (Winter, 1970), 144–149.

Roeder, George. "The Image of the Mexican." Unpub. MSS, University of Wisconsin, 1971.

Rowland, Donald W. *History of the Office of the Coordinator of Inter-American Affairs.* Washington, D.C., 1947.

Sarmiento, D. F. *Life in the Argentine Republic in the Days of the Tyrants.* New York, 1868.

Sennett, Ted. *Warner Brothers Presents.* New York, 1971.

Solanas, Fernando E., and Octavio Getino. *Cine, cultura, y descolonización.* Buenos Aires, 1973.

Steinbeck, John. *Viva Zapata!* New York, 1975.

Thomas, Tony, and Jim Terry. *The Busby Berkeley Book.* New York, 1973.

Wood, Bryce. *The Making of the Good Neighbor Policy.* New York, 1961.

Zinman, David. *Saturday Afternoon at the Bijou.* New York, 1973.

INDEX